CURIOUS TALES
❋ from ❋
West Yorkshire

CURIOUS TALES

from

West Yorkshire

Howard Peach

The History Press

in Wakefield. For help with illustrations I am most grateful to the following: Anne Slater; Bradford Libraries, Archives and Information Services; the Marks & Spencer Company Archive; and the Yorkshire Waterways Museum.

From talking to people across the old West Riding it is clear that so many historic and intriguing artefacts are unfamiliar. I hope this book does something to raise awareness and prompt further research for us all.

Howard Peach, 2010

☙ A ❧

ACCIDENTS

During the early nineteenth century it was said that no whole man existed in Skelmanthorpe, as all workers had lost toes, fingers, ears, noses, arms etc in the hand looms.

In 1808, at St George's church, Doncaster, a bell ringer, John Smith, was swept up by his rope to the belfry chamber top. His injuries from the fall were fatal.

In 1878, Arthur Standidge, rector of Adel church, fell through the top deck of his three-decker pulpit while delivering a sermon; it was quickly replaced by a safe single-decker.

'A portion of the school wall was broken down through five bullocks trying to enter the gate at once.' (Log book, Thorner C.E. School, 27 January 1934.)

An old saying in mining areas like Castleford was, 'When tha seed lav door were missin', tha knowed some collier were dead'.

ACKWORTH PLAGUE STONE

During the seventeenth century there were many outbreaks of plague. In nearby Pontefract in 1603, 228 people had died. The hollow on top of the rounded stone on Castle Syke Hill is where fearful villagers left money in vinegar (hoping to disinfect it) in exchange for food and medicines during the bubonic plague of 1645. Despite these precautions, 153 villagers perished. Hepworth Feast, near Holmfirth, is held on the last Monday of June with a band-led procession to commemorate their plague of 1665.

AFTER YOU, PATRICK

Immediately after his wedding to Maria Branwell at Guiseley church, on 19 December 1812, the Revd Patrick Brontë (future father of the three famous novelist daughters) swapped roles and performed a similar ceremony for his friend, the Revd William Morgan, who was marrying Maria's cousin.

A Regency engraving of St George's church, Doncaster.

ALL IN THE DAY'S WALK

West Yorkshire has produced some prodigious walkers: 'About the year 1736 Richard Wilson, a resident of Ossett, made two pieces of broadcloth; he carried one of them on his head to Leeds and sold it – the merchant being in want of the fellow piece, he went from Leeds to Ossett, then carried the other piece to Leeds, and then walked to Ossett again; he walked about forty miles that day'. (John Mayhall: *Annals and History of Leeds*, 1860.) From her farm at Haworth, Nancy Ickringill carried woollen pieces to Halifax market. In so doing she damaged her shoulder and walked lopsidedly. Levi Whitehead (1687-1787) was a fast runner, covering four miles in nineteen minutes. At ninety-six he was still doing his daily four miles around the Bramham area.

ALMSHOUSES FOR THE MIDDLE CLASSES

Under the will of Christopher Tancred, a hospital at Whixley Hall opened in 1762 for gentlemen pensioners – ex-army officers, clergy, decayed nobility, the first of whom was Sir Charles Sedley. They were often badly behaved, throwing food, entertaining women in their rooms and fighting. Some, it was found, had wives, so they lost their places. The residents were catered for by a warden/chaplain, a cook and three maids. By 1871 only three remained, so the Hall closed.

In 1754, when Tancred died, aged sixty-four, his coffin was hung in chains on the north wall of the Hall. Eventually it was moved to a cellar, then transferred to the vault under the chapel and finally to the church.

From his will of 1867 (he died in 1870 leaving an estate of £60,000), a John Abbott's Trustees Ladies' Home was created for ladies of good birth and education now living in reduced circumstances as widows or spinsters (and of fifty years of age or more). The Home was situated in Skircoat, 'in that part of the borough of Halifax most affected for residences of the best class…' Each had to have at least £20 income: none had more than £100. Elected by trustees, there were twelve occupants who lived in, and sixty recipients, non-resident, who were given between £12 and £20 annually. While the Halifax area was preferred, there was no religious discrimination. If any lady married she had to go.

ANTI-CLERICAL CHARTIST

A prominent Chartist, Ben Rushton, a Halifax handloom weaver and Methodist preacher, made an impassioned speech at a Whit Monday Rally at Peep Green in 1839 accusing the clergy of being far too passive in standing up for workers' rights: 'They preached Christ and a crust, passive obedience and non-resistance. Let the people keep from those churches and chapels... Let them go to those men who preached Christ and a full belly, Christ and a well-clothed back, Christ and a good house to live in – Christ and Universal Suffrage'. Such words were not calculated to endear him to any part of the Establishment – and the Chapel duly expelled him.

ANTI-RAIL RHODES

In 1840, on the eve of great railway developments, the vicar of Hebden Bridge, the Revd J.A. Rhodes, insisted that the new railway station be sited at least one mile from his home in Mytholmroyd: not for him the additional rewarding challenge of a mission station on his doorstep.

ARCHBISHOP INDULGENT

In 1233 Archbishop Walter de Gray of York offered indulgences to all repentant sinners who contributed to the building at 'Werreby' (Wetherby) of a new bridge over the River Wharfe.

ASKERN SPA

Situated near Doncaster and an erstwhile mining area, Askern hardly seems likely to have offered facilities to rival Harrogate or Buxton. Back in the 1700s the waters' noxious odours and taste were noted by a Dr Short in a book called *Mineral Waters of Yorkshire*. When healing properties were claimed, bath houses appeared; by 1880 there were five. As visitors flocked by rail, new guest houses appeared. But then new seams of coal were discovered, and as mining took over and men with blackened faces and homely accents emerged from the pit, spa clientele somehow declined.

Ossett, too, had short-lived Spa ambitions. A local stonemason developed two bathing houses in the 1820s, attracting sufferers from gout, rheumatism and scrofula. The south-east area of the town is still known as Ossett Spa.

AUDIENCE PARTICIPATION

During the 1860s, in the Bradford Theatre Royal, where a rougher element was generally well represented, interludes were sometimes enlivened by lowering a reluctant kicking man from the gallery to the orchestra pit.

Mayflower Flag, St Helena's church, Austerfield.

William Bradford Memorial, St Helena's churchyard, Austerfield.

AUSTERFIELD

Here was the birthplace of William Bradford, born of yeomen farming stock at Austerfield Manor and baptised in St Helena's church on 19 March 1589. (The Puritanical history of the church is slightly compromised by a rare Sheila-na-gig on the most easterly pillar on the north side of the nave, i.e. a quasi-erotic carving of a naked lady – a fertility symbol? A warning against lust?)

A sickly child, William became a devout Bible student. At nearby Scrooby his great mentor and ally William Brewster lived in the manor house, which was used as a meeting place for sympathisers who found oppressive the requirement to worship in the Anglican Church. Becoming religious asylum seekers, they went to Holland in 1607; and in 1620 over a hundred of these separatists sailed, as Pilgrim Fathers, in the *Mayflower*, seeking a fresh start and a new religious identity. The following year William Bradford became Governor of Plymouth Colony, Massachusetts.

BACON AND BUTTIES BET

On the 11 May 1818, 'David Addy Junior for a small Wager agreed to Eat Four Pounds of Bacon Fryed in one hower which he Completed 10 minutes under the Time Given and Danced a Single Dance after and Eat some Cheese and Bread after'. (Diary of Ecclesfield villager from 1775 to 1845, edited by Thomas Winder in 1922.)

On a common-sense basis one might suppose that a workhouse would be among the last institutions to burgle. Anyway, someone-in-the-know decided to break and enter Ecclesfield Workhouse Pantery (sic) in December 1820 to steal over fourteen pounds in cash, doubtless with a view to celebrate Christmas.

BAREFOOT AT BRIG'US

Brass bands like the Black Dyke Mills of Queensbury, Bradford, have won enormous prestige in West Yorkshire – and indeed nationally. Others, fractionally less well known, acquired their own reputations: the Pomfret (Pontefract) Victoria Brass Band was known as the Ale and Bacca Band – no doubt for good reason.

There has always been an independent spirit about Brighouse which, for instance, proclaims a red rose on its coat-of-arms! A story goes that one night the famous Brighouse and Rastrick Band was returning home with a trophy. It was late, and they didn't want their marching feet from the station to spoil the sleep of their townsfolk (removing their shoes to avoid this) – but they decided to play a celebratory air *'See the Conquering Hero Comes'* as they went! In 1977 the band's version of *The Floral Dance* rose to number two in the charts.

BARRING OUT

On Shrove Tuesday, in some schools, children let off steam by barring out their teachers until a holiday was granted. Such breaks from routine were not usually threatening. Indeed, they were often accompanied by jollity and ginger parkin. But during the eighteenth century there were serious scholastic disturbances around the country, as in Manchester, Birmingham, Coventry and Shrewsbury. At Doncaster Grammar School on 15 January 1730 boyish spirits rose too high and windows were smashed. The Corporation footed the bill but declared that the head, Edmund Withers, should not be 'tyed from correcting the Boys'. These were difficult times: his salary was often in arrears.

BATH NIGHT

Saturday evening used to be a hearthside family bathing ritual. The oldest child went first into the tin bath, which was heated up with boiler water, supplemented by occasional fireback kettles. By the time it was the youngest's turn, the water might be a touch grimey. Until you reached teenage years, though, it was companionable, especially afterwards, sitting around in warm towels.

BATTLES

It is curious indeed that three decisive battles should have been fought but a few miles apart. The Battle of Wakefield, 30 December 1460, centring on Sandal Castle, might have been a siege, but the Lancastrians taunted the Yorkists to show themselves. Richard of York's severed head was mounted on Micklegate Bar, York. This was so 'York may overlook the town of York,' in Lancastrian Queen Margaret's poetic words (according, of course, to Shakespeare's *Henry VI*, III.I.IV).

Did the mocking song *The Grand Old Duke of York* originate here? An alternative claim is that the song started at Allerton Park in the 1790s when the indecisive Frederick Augustus, Duke of York (and second son of George III), marched his soldiers up and down a mound as some sort of preparation against the French. The creation of the mound itself, by men with spades and wheelbarrows, was pointless.

At Towton, near Tadcaster, on Palm Sunday of the 29 March 1461, Edward of York (son of the above Richard) defeated the Lancastrians supporting Henry VI and his ambitious Queen Margaret of Anjou. There were mutilations on both sides. It was said that the River Cock was swollen with melting snow and blood. St Mary's church at Lead sheltered some of the wounded. This time it was Lancastrian heads that were mounted on Micklegate. Lord Dacre, a Lancastrian leader struck down as he took wine, was buried astride his horse in the churchyard of Saxton All Saints.

During the Civil War, just north at Marston Moor, on 2–3 July 1644 Cromwell's Ironsides defeated the Royalists under Prince Rupert (nephew of Charles I). Thomas Fairfax, Parliamentary commander, ensured York's decent surrender without reprisals or vandalism – for which the grateful city gave him a butt of sack and a tun of French wine.

BEATING THE BOUNDS

In some communities, the Rogationtide or rammalation (corruption of 'perambulation') custom continues of encouraging children to walk the village boundaries. Holy Thursday was also a favoured day. Parents, parish priest and churchwardens carrying willow wands of office led the walk to impress on youngsters the importance of maintaining parish boundaries. There was a good deal of horseplay, like a slap or a bump to impress some feature like stone or stile, with compensatory refreshments provided from church funds at the end of the walk. At Halifax in 1770 a stone bridge, predecessor of the Old North Bridge, collapsed during the walk. Enclosures militated against such communal activities. At Shelley, near Huddersfield, bounds are beaten on New Year's Day, participants being known as Shelley Welly Walkers. Around Adel, a fifteen mile walk takes place in May on Rogation Sunday; and a less strenuous one in June from St Peter's church, Thorner.

BLACK-FACED CLOCK

The date is uncertain, but Ripponden folk are fond of the fable of St Bartholomew's church clock. Two faces were cleaned, but one side of the parish (Barkisland) refused to contribute. Their clock face stayed black.

Micklegate Bar as it appeared at the beginning of
the nineteenth century.

Towton Cross on the battlefield site.

Lord Dacre's tomb, Saxton. The white pyramid marks the remains of unknown soldiers found at Towton
Hall, 1996.

'BLOODY POMFRET'

So-called in Shakespeare's *Richard II*, that monarch, having been held captive in the castle, died mysteriously in 1400. Shakespeare made out that the king was struck down by Sir Piers Exton... or was he starved to death?

Thomas of Lancaster was beheaded here in 1322 after defeat at Boroughbridge and trial before Edward II, his cousin. Thomas had been responsible for the execution of Piers Gaveston, the former royal favourite.

In Shakespeare's *King John*, a hermit, Peter of Pomfret, is brought in to predict the king's downfall (Act IV, Scene ii). When John learns that French troops are massing for attack he orders Peter's imprisonment.

One castle dungeon was carved out of a rock and the luckless prisoners thrown in through a hole in the roof.

BODY SNATCHERS

Exhuming recent corpses and selling them to medical students in Edinburgh became a macabre yet lucrative trade. In March 1826 Martha Oddy (who died aged just fifteen) was dug up in Armley churchyard. In this case the corpse was retrieved and reburied in the original grave. For this offence Michael Armstrong was sentenced at Leeds Sessions to six months in York Castle.

Various expedients were adopted to deter 'resurrectionists '. In High Bradfield churchyard, west of Sheffield, a watch tower was built.

BRADFORD RESOLUTION, 1825

The Bradford Board of Commissioners resolved that 'the hog-stye in Manningham Lane opposite Christ church and the muck-heap opposite Rawson Place be removed, and that Thomas Hoadley's pigs be not allowed to run loose and be fed in the Market Place'.

BRADFORD FIRSTS

It is curious how often Bradford led the country in child welfare. Through Margaret McMillan, the Wapping Street School gained the first school baths in England in 1897; school medical inspections and open-air nurseries followed. Inspectors found that about one-third of youngsters were sewn into their clothes, which were not removed until winter was over, hence the lice problem! School meals were introduced in 1906. Interestingly, Jonathon Priestley, headmaster of Green Lane School, Manningham and father of the future novelist J.B.P., was at this time active in promoting school and adult welfare. Green Lane was first school to establish a school meals depot, supplying meals to needy children elsewhere.

England's first temperance society formed here in 1830, aimed particularly at youngsters' self-control regarding drink. But it is odd also that Bradford was the last to have its own municipal hospital; it also managed to retain its trolley-buses until 1972.

Watch-house, St Nicholas churchyard, Upper Bradfield.

White Abbey Feeding Centre, Bradford, 1908. The man on the right is Jonathon Priestley, headmaster of Green Lane School and father of the novelist. (Courtesy of Bradford Libraries).

BRADFORD PALS

Among the early volunteers to enlist in 1914 were hundreds of young men from West Yorkshire who have gone down in history as 'Pals' – Leeds Pals, Barnsley Pals, Sheffield – aye, an' Hull, too. They chummed up from the same areas, often the same streets. Theirs is a heroic story.

In the early months of the First World War some 2,000 young Bradford men from all classes – apprentices, wool sorters, lads from mills, mines and offices – took the king's shilling and volunteered to fight against Germany. They formed the 16th and 18th Battalions of the West Yorkshire Regiment. At about 7.30 on the morning of 1 July 1916 they left the comparative security of the trenches to cross No Man's Land, their objective being to capture the village of Serre. The German machine gunners mowed them down. An hour later 1,770 had been killed or injured, and no gains made. Such was the awesome start to the Battle of the Somme. The Sheffield Pals lost fewer – but far too many.

Private Arthur Pearson of Leeds escaped when a bullet hit his bully beef tin.

The Bradford Pals Memorial stands in Centenary Square, and there is a window to their memory in the cathedral.

How the *Illustrated London News* depicted the first wave of British troops at the Somme.

German prisoners walking down a trench at the Somme, whilst 'Tommy' looks on.

Bramhope Railway Tunnel Memorial, Otley.

BRAMHOPE TUNNEL

Adjacent to Otley All Saints' churchyard is this unusual monument, a crenellated stone replica of the northern entrance of the Bramhope tunnel on the Leeds-Thirsk railway. Between 1845 and 1849 twenty-three navvies were killed during the construction of the tunnel, which was 2 miles 243 yards long, and up to 290ft deep. Some 2,300 navvies and 400 horses were employed. The work was beset by many problems – rock falls, subsidence, floods, etc. Many families were encamped in small huts in the area. The men consumed prodigious amounts of meat, bread and ale – five quarts a day was not unusual. So alcohol was a special problem, causing absenteeism and violence. A riot ensued when supplies were cut off by the contractors.

BRANWELL'S LAMP

Charlotte Nicholls (nee Brontë) was in the habit of placing in the window of her matrimonial study at Haworth a lamp to guide homewards the sometimes unsteady footsteps of her bibulous brother Branwell, returning from the Black Bull and the hospitality of landlord Thomas Sugden (who doubtless saw him as valuable curiosity). Sometimes he re-entered through the back door if his father, the Revd Patrick, was on the prowl.

Branwell was employed as a booking clerk at Luddenden Foot station, lodging at the Lord Nelson Inn, until he lost his job in March 1842 owing to careless accounting fuelled by drink (and also by opium bought from Betty Hardacre's drug shop, opposite the Black Bull). In October 1843 he wrote to the Church trustees to refute local gossip that the lotion he was using for weak eyesight smelled like alcohol. Two years later he was sacked as tutor to the Robinson family at Thorp Green, accused of an affair with the lady of the house.

Like his sisters, he died young – a failed though talented artist.

BREWERIES IMBROGLIO

Rivalries in the Smith family evolved into an extremely complicated history, far too difficult to summarise here. It seems safe to record that from 1758 Tadcaster brewing rested mainly with the Hartley family. From the 1850s there was a take-over by the Smith family with the names John, Samuel and William to the fore. But disputes arose, and in 1884 William built a New Brewery next door, which is the basis of the modern John Smith's. The Old Brewery was redeveloped by a younger Samuel Smith, whose name remains and whose brewery dray horses are still seen on Tadcaster streets. But separate development needs to be stressed!

BRIDGE CHANTRY CHAPELS

The West Riding has two of England's four (the others being at St Ives, Cambridgeshire; and at Bradford-on-Avon). Chantry comes from the old French, *chanterie* – offering a daily mass for the soul of the founder or patron. It was once a stopping place for medieval travellers.

Wakefield's chapel, over the River Calder, was built in the middle of the fourteenth century. Following the Tudor Dissolution, and before its restoration in 1848, the building was used as a warehouse, tailor's, library and cheesecake shop.

Chantry Chapel, Rotherham.   John Smith's Brewery, Tadcaster.

Rotherham's chapel over the Don was funded in 1483 by John Bokyng, a schoolmaster, who was probably helped by Thomas Rotherham, later Archbishop of York. After the Dissolution it served as a sixteenth-century almshouse, a jail from 1779, then as a hospital, and from 1888 as a newspaper/tobacconist's. It was restored and rededicated in 1924.

BRODSWORTH HALL AND BLEAK HOUSE

Charles Sabine Thelluson built the country house (1860-71) on the eventual proceeds of his father's will, which was disputed for sixty years until the House of Lords gave a ruling. The case provided the model for Dickens' Jarndyce v Jarndyce in *Bleak House*, satirising the contortedly slow processes of the Court of Chancery.

BRONTË BELLS

What a difference a year can make in literary fortunes! When, in 1846, Currer, Ellis and Acton Bell published their first tentative poems, only two copies were sold. But the following year saw the publication and continuing success of *Jane Eyre* by Charlotte Brontë, after a year of rejections, as well as *Wuthering Heights* (Emily) and *Agnes Grey* (Anne).

Curiosities abounded with the sisters. They were small – Emily was the tallest at just 5ft. Despite their passionate depths, socially they often appeared shy and introverted.

In some circles *Jane Eyre* caused a furore. Not only did this brave, loyal, strong and independent heroine look to meet men on equal emotional terms, but she also won the love and respect of Mr Rochester, finally gaining ascendancy over this blind and scarred husband. For some of her female contemporaries this was too much. Lady Elizabeth Eastlake declared 'the tone of the mind and thought which has overthrown authority and violated every code human and divine abroad, and fostered Chartism and rebellion at home, is the same which has also written *Jane Eyre*'.

Much discouragement had already been overcome. In March 1837 Charlotte had received a letter from the Poet Laureate, Robert Southey, asserting 'Literature cannot be the business of a woman's life; and it ought not to be.'

We know better in Yorkshire!

BULL-BAITING

Until 1835, bull baiting, thought to enhance the meat's tenderness and flavour, was a legal requirement prior to slaughter. The animal was chained in the market place and set upon by dogs. In Keighley the venue was at Church Green; at Almondbury on the Common – the last occasion (August 1824) accompanied by a rush-bearing ceremony. Defaulters were prosecuted. On 5 May 1752 Benjamin Shires was fined 3s 4d for selling unbaited beef at Skipton (where the bull ring was outside the Bay Horse Inn).

BUSLINGTHORPE

A district of Leeds, about a mile north of the city centre. The name contains thirteen different letters. Any advance anywhere?

BYNG (1742-1813) BANGS ON

Diarist, grumbler, ex-Guards officer and later the 5th Viscount Torrington, Byng was notoriously fastidious: 'The Angel Inn where I expected everything comfortable, I found to be nasty and insolent. In a sad room, after my long ride, I could not eat what they brought which was a dirty bit of salmon with two lumps of boiled beef. I sent them both out and then could not get a waiter near me. I longed to be able to kick the landlord to whom I complained in vain'. (The Hon. John Byng writing on 2 June 1792 at Doncaster.)

At Rotherham, the Crown Inn was reputedly the best, but 'a more dreary, blacker, tumbledown, old casemented ruin co'ud not be… shatter'd beds, windows broken, paper hanging down, blankets and curtains torn…'

Skipton he described as 'this nasty, filthily inhabited town; for I never saw more slatterns; or dirtier houses'.

CASTLEFORD RHYME

'Castleford maids must needs be fair,
For they wash in Calder and rinse in Aire.'
A compliment for those pre-piped water days!

CAT'S EYES

The invention of Percy Shaw (1890-1976) was inspired by girlfriend troubles. His brother persuaded him to leave the Halifax belles, and pursue his love life in Bradford. Percy found, however, that driving home at night down the steep and unlit Queensbury Road was dangerous. The reflection of headlights in tramlines was one starting point for the future; being startled by a live cat's eyes staring at him through the fog was another. Surreptitiously, Percy experimented on various roads with fairy lights, central metal strips and intrusions of glass marbles. Experiments were refined and in 1934 the invention was patented. Finally, Reflecting Road Studs Ltd. was set up in an old stable in his native Boothtown. Percy's first order was from Baildon Council: three dozen cats eyes for 3s 9d. The Second World War and the blackout gave the invention mighty impetus, and fame and money were won.

But Percy continued to live rather frugally, and unmarried, in the same uncarpeted house – cheerless except for three television sets constantly running on different channels. Although he bought himself a Rolls Royce motor car, he rarely left Yorkshire (except to receive the OBE in 1965).

CHARITIES

A Dole Ceremony is conducted at Penistone town hall on Good Friday when the mayor gives out sixty bags of flour. The Dole stems from Tudor times; by William Turton's will, rye flour was to be given to the poor on this day.

On May Days at Wath-on-Dearne Tom Tuke used to throw bread buns to the assembled poor from the top of All Saints' church tower.

During the first part of the nineteenth century at Todmorden, the Gartside Charity provided poor families with lengths of linen at Christmas and New Year to use as sheets and clothing.

CHILD'S PLAY

'The two small playgrounds are covered with rough boiler clinker.' (County Medical Officer's report, Old Sharlston School, Crofton, near Ackworth, in 1906.)

CHILD SLAVES AND FEMALE COLLIERS

'I visited the Hunshelf Colliery on the eighteenth of January; it is a day pit: that is, there is no shaft or descent; the gate or entrance is at the side of a bank, and nearly horizontal. The gate was not more than a yard high, and in some places not above two feet. When I arrived at the board, or workings of the pit, I found at one of the

Female pit labourer, c. 1840.

Silkstone monument.

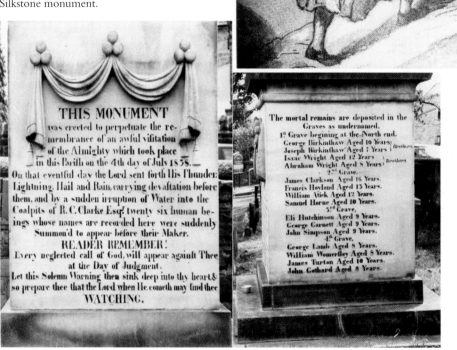

THIS MONUMENT

was erected to perpetuate the re-
membrance of an awful visitation
of the Almighty which took place
in this Parish on the 4th day of July 1838.
On that eventful day the Lord sent forth His Thunder:
Lightning, Hail and Rain, carrying devastation before
them, and by a sudden irruption of Water into the
Coalpits of R. C. Clarke Esq.ᵗ twenty six human be-
ings whose names are recorded here were suddenly
Summon'd to appear before their Maker.

READER REMEMBER!

Every neglected call of God, will appear against Thee
at the Day of Judgment.
Let this Solemn Warning then sink deep into thy heart,&
so prepare thee that the Lord when He cometh may find thee
WATCHING.

The mortal remains are deposited in the
Graves as undernamed,
1ˢᵗ Grave begining at the North end.
George Birkinthaw Aged 10 Years ⎱ Brothers
Joseph Birkinthaw Aged 7 Years ⎰
Isaac Wright Aged 12 Years ⎱ Brothers
Abraham Wright Aged 8 Years ⎰
2ⁿᵈ Grave.
James Clarkson Aged 16 Years.
Francis Hoyland Aged 13 Years.
William Atick Aged 12 Years.
Samuel Horne Aged 10 Years.
3ʳᵈ Grave.
Eli Hutchinson Aged 9 Years.
George Garnett Aged 9 Years.
John Simpson Aged 9 Years.
4ᵗʰ Grave.
George Lamb Aged 8 Years.
William Womerfley Aged 8 Years.
James Turton Aged 10 Years.
John Gothard Aged 8 Years.

side-boards down a narrow passage a girl of fourteen years of age in boy's clothes, picking down the coal with the regular pick used by the men. She was half sitting, half lying at her work, and said she found it tired her very much, and "of course she didn't like it". The place where she was at work was not two feet high… No less than six girls out of eighteen men and children are employed in this pit.'

'The men work in a state of perfect nakedness, and are in this state assisted in their labour by females of all ages, from girls of six years old to women of twenty-one, these females themselves quite naked down to the waist.'

Betty Wardle reported: 'I have worked in a pit since I was six years old. I have had four children, two of them were born while I worked in the pits. I worked in the pits whilst I was in the family way. I had a child born in the pits, and I brought it up in the pit shaft in my skirt.' (*Report on Women and Children's Labour in Mines*, 1842).

At Mitchell's Worsted Mill at Keighley in the 1840s an overseer's strap was embedded with six nails.

Despite the 1842 Coal Mines Act some women and girls continued to work underground. Five years later Patience Wroe (nine) was still working in Caphouse Colliery as a hurrier, pulling baskets or even tubs of coal.

CHILDREN'S DEATHS

The monument in All Saints' churchyard at Silkstone lists twenty-six children, aged seven to seventeen, who drowned in the Huskar mine during a storm on 4 July 1838. They were caught while trying to climb out of a ventilation shaft. The enormity of the tragedy led to Lord Ashley's bill of 1842 to prevent women and children working in mines.

CHIMNEY CLEANING

Interesting suggestions for chimney cleaning have included pushing up lighted papers or small amounts of gunpowder in a rolled-up paper fuse, or dropping a hen down from the roof.

CHOCS AWAY

During the 1919-20 football season Bradford City were beaten away in an FA cup match with Bristol City. Later some team members admitted that a pre-game visit to Fry's chocolate factory, though sustaining, might have been unwise…

'The Chocolate Club delivery gave us a fright. As usual the good old railway got the blame. Rats at Barnsley got some of our chocs.' (Parish Magazine, Ryhill, December 1925.)

CHURCH CLYPPING

Clyppan comes from Old English – to clasp, embrace. After an indoor service the congregation and choir process outside and surround the church, joining hands in a symbolic chain as prayers are intoned to bless the church and ward off evil. A hymn commonly sung is, 'We love the place, O God'. Clypping was revived in 1906 at St Oswald's church, Guiseley, at an August patronal festival; and from 1926 has taken place in July at St Peter's church, Tankersley.

Another outdoors church occasion takes place at St John's, Baildon on Ascension morning, when hymns are sung from the tower and then in the churchyard.

CHURCHWARDENS' ACCOUNTS

These records illustrate many aspects of parish life in times past.

Bradfield Parish church:

1630: 'given to a poor person by consent towards buying a cow – x s'.

1631: 'Edward Broomhead for one and a half years' wage dog whipping – xvi d.' (Farmers in particular were in the habit of bringing their dogs into church. The animal sometimes disturbed the parson's sermon, though not always his sleeping master.)

Clypping ceremony, St Peter's church, Tankersley.

All Saints, Rotherham:

a) 1706, 2s 'to George Ellis's wife to buy her mother's winding sheet.'

b) 1711, £24 'for treating My Lord Archbishop of York.' (Must have been quite a parish party!)

At St Oswald's church, Yeadon, in 1723, John Hainsworth recorded '6d for ringers ale; for foxhead 1s 0d; foumard 4d; given for getting the Boggard – 1s 0d'. (A foumard was a polecat. Churchwardens rewarded parishioners who brought in dead vermin. 'Boggard' suggests the paranormal – an unwelcome spirit, a ghost, possibly that of a dog. We can but wonder.)

1757, Heptonstall: 'For making clock face fast when near blown of in winds... 2s 6d.'

In 1799, Slaithwaite churchwardens spent 7s on wood for a 'cuck stool' and 3s for wood for a whipping post. (The cuckstool, though very likely a ducking stool, could also have been a tumbril for public humiliation of an offender.)

CINEMA TRAGEDY

In the Public Hall, Barnsley, on 11 January 1908, nine girls and seven boys were killed in a staircase crush after being told they could go to the pit stalls for their penny entrance fee. The coroner decided that an attendant, William Rain, had been negligent in sending them down. The tragedy led to tighter regulations in the Cinema Act (1909).

South Gatehouse, Skipton Castle. 'Desormais' (henceforth) was the motto of the Cliffords, i.e. here we stay!

Pontefract's motto: 'After the death of the father, we are for the son'.

CIVIL WAR CURIOSITIES

Many and various claims have been made for the temporary lodgings of soldiers. Did Gunthwaite barn really accommodate Cromwell's Ironsides several times?

In 1644, on the eve of the battle of Marston Moor, Cromwell's soldiers took over the Black Bull, Otley and drank it dry.

The parish church of St Peter (now Bradford Cathedral) was protected from Royalist cannon by bales of wool hung from the tower. During the siege of 1643 Lady Fairfax was taken hostage in the High Street, but was very soon returned to her husband, Sir Thomas, by the opposition. She was transported in the Earl of Newcastle's own carriage.

In contrast is the legend of 'Pity poor Bradford': while William Cavendish, Earl of Newcastle slept in Bolling Hall in July 1643, a ghost visited him in a dream and beseeched, 'Pity poor Bradford!' Hitherto Newcastle had intended a massacre of the townsfolk. Accordingly, however, although the town was sacked and pillaged the citizenry was largely spared. There had been some provocation: parliamentary defenders had been ruthless with Royalist prisoners, giving no quarter (hence the expression 'Bradford Quarter').

On 1st November 1643, during skirmishes at Heptonstall, attacking Cavaliers took no account of a raging storm, and many were swept away. Others were crushed by boulders rolled down on them by defending Roundheads. Later Royalist reprisals included the burning of houses.

Re the siege of Pontefract Castle: 'April 6 1645, The enemy basely stayed all wine coming to the castle for serving of the Communion upon Easter Day, although Forbus (Parliamentary Commander) had graunted protecktion for the same, and one Browne of Wakefield said if it were for our damnation we should have it, but not for our salvation.' (Diary of Nathan Drake.)

When the news of the execution of Charles I reached Pontefract the Royalist garrison, under Colonel John Morris, proclaimed Charles' son as King Charles II. No other town ventured to do so. New coins were quickly minted, inscribed '*Post Mortem Patris Pro Filio*': 'after the death of the father we are for the son' (hence the town's motto). Morris had to surrender the castle, but escaped – only to be recaptured later and hanged, drawn and quartered at York.

The Roundhead siege of Skipton Castle lasted for three years, the Royalists surrendering in December 1645. But they were allowed a triumphal march down the High Street with colours flying, and to disperse safely.

CIVIL WEDDINGS

During the Cromwellian Commonwealth after the Civil War, banns were called in the market place, not in church. Elizabeth Appleyard and Thomas Rogerson were joined in matrimony in an Otley alehouse on 15 June 1652 by Mr Precious, JP. As parish clerk, the bride's dismayed father, Robert Appleyard, had withheld his consent.

CLERK IN UNHOLY ORDERS

In 1650 the constables and churchwardens of Kirkburton and the Chapelry of Holmfirth organised a petition for the creation of a parish in Holmfirth. In support, William Hepworth, clerk in orders at Kirkburton, pressurised non-attenders at Holmfirth into paying 2d each for the building of a new church/chapel. He threatened them with 'mischief if it lyed in his power'.

LADY ANNE CLIFFORD (1590-1676)

Despite the slighting of Skipton Castle at the end of the Civil War, the building was put under repair only a few years later by Lady Anne Clifford, who had spent heavily on lawsuits to gain her inheritance. Many tales are told of her generosity. Murgatroyd, a rich Halifax clothier, acquired land nearby (*see* East Riddlesden Hall) for which he owed one hen per year to Lady Anne. However, the clothier refused to pay. She won that litigation too, and when the hen was handed over she invited her opponent to a banquet: the food she served included the disputed poultry! Yet even she was affected by some of the superstitions of the age, burning her nail parings so that witches could not use them.

Slant Gate is a steep street at Kirkburton.

CLIMBING BOY TRAGEDY

On 13 May 1832 eight year-old John Wigglesworth got stuck in a chimney flue at Dr Gilby's house, Wakefield. When rescue attempts failed, the sweep, Thomas Blanco, partially dismantled the chimney, but the boy had suffocated.

Master sweeps often treated their 'apprentices' cruelly, beating them, hardening the youngsters' elbows and knees with salt water, and using the threat of fire to force them up soot-choked and narrow flues. The loathsome trade was not stopped until 1875, despite the efforts of such social reformers as James Montgomery (who in 1824 had published his *Chimney Sweepers' Friend and Climbing Boys Album*, highlighting the plight of youngsters like seven-year old Francis O'Neill, kidnapped from a Sheffield workhouse and forced to sweep chimneys before becoming seriously ill – whereupon he was thrown out to starve).

What irony resides in the fact that Montgomery, also a famous hymn writer, penned the words of the carol, 'Angels from the Realms of Glory' – a spiritual vision sharply contrasting with the brutal realities that daily confronted babes like John Wigglesworth and Francis O'Neill.

COAL CARRYING CHAMPIONSHIP

These events have drawn crowds to Gawthorpe (Ossett) every Easter Monday since 1963. Youngsters race first, carrying small bags of coal; then women take over, carrying 50lb sacks; and finally men struggle with 100lb burdens. The race, over 1,100 yards, starts at the Royal Oak Inn, Owl Lane and finishes at the Maypole on the village green. The winners are hailed King and Queen of the Coil Umpers and receive large sums of money. David Jones of Meltham won the race in 1991 and 1995 in four minutes and six seconds. It all arose from pub banter between a coal merchant and a pal about personal fitness, resulting in a challenge as to who could 'carry a bag o' coil fothest.' So the invitation was extended.

COCK THROWING

With a rooster tethered to a post, a competitor was allowed to throw a stick, or a broom handle, from twenty yards or so, and could claim the bird if he knocked it down and it didn't get up before retrieval. The game took on piquancy when cockerels became skilled at dodging missiles. This was a favoured blood sport on Shrove Tuesday in Sheffield during the eighteenth and early nineteenth centuries.

A worthy attempt by the Sheffield authorities in 1751 to draw spectators away from watching cock fights was to enlist a number of local cricketers to offer healthier entertainment. Success was incomplete. The initiative was probably due to William Hogarth's recent depiction of the barbarous activity in *'The Four Stages of Cruelty'*.

COINCIDENCES

Todmorden has produced two Nobel Laureates: Sir John Cockroft, for his work on splitting the atom, which gained the Nobel Prize for Physics in 1951; and Professor Geoffrey Wilkinson, honoured in 1973 for his researches in chemistry.

Coal-carrying race, Gawthorpe.

Wilfred Rhodes (1877-1973) and George Hirst (1871-1954) both came from Kirkheaton, near Huddersfield. Both batted right handed and bowled left arm. Both achieved phenomenal records. In 1900 Wilfred took 261 wickets at an average of 13.81. In a long career he took 4,204 first class wickets, played in tests for over thirty-two years, the last at the age of fifty-two in Kingston, Jamaica, and batted in every position from one to eleven.

Also a celebrated England player, George made the highest score in county cricket, 341, versus Leicestershire in 1905. The following year he not only completed the double (i.e. a thousand runs and a hundred wickets), but also scored 2,385 runs and took 208 wickets.

In the replay for the FA Cup in 1911 Bradford enjoyed a double success: City finally beat Newcastle United 1-0, and the brand new trophy duly returned to the town where it had just been designed by local jewellers, Messrs Fettorini.

COLLAPSES

On 3 Feb 1916 a pillar supporting two arches of the Penistone viaduct fell into the River Don. A locomotive dropped too, but miraculously it was recovered and persuaded to work for many years!

On 1 November 1965 three of Ferrybridge's eight cooling towers collapsed in high winds.

On 19 March 1969 the 1,265ft high Emley Moor television mast collapsed owing to ice deposits on the support wires.

COLLINGHAM ROBBERS

The story is told of two Collingham horsemen who, in 1674, broke into Harden Hall, Bingley to rob Samuel Sunderland of some of his gold. In order to divert possible pursuers, their steeds had horseshoes nailed on back to front. But the dog taken carelessly with them was left behind; and, of course, it led the law straight to one of the villains' homes as they were counting the loot. After due trial at York they were hanged. Their innocent apprentice was obliged to carry out the sentence, and was so disturbed by it that he throttled himself.

COLLOP MONDAY

The day before Shrove Tuesday was the penultimate occasion for eating collops – any leftover piece of meat or bacon – before the Lenten Fast. Or so the theory went. So there was often a considerable fry-up and general feasting. Some shopkeepers gave sweets to children, as at Meltham.

CORN RIOTS

The high price of bread led to riots in Halifax on 7 June 1783. The Corn Market was the centre of attacks which had to be put down by soldiers. A ringleader was Thomas Spencer, one of the notorious Cragg Vale coiners, who impulsively demanded that the master of the Boar's Head Inn should sell his grain cheaply to the starving poor. On refusal the mob attacked the corn wagons at a nearby warehouse. Other wagons were seized elsewhere in the town.

A Heptonstall youth, Mark Sattonstall, was arrested as an accomplice ringleader. After being tried, the pair were hanged on Beacon Hill, Halifax on 16 August, in front of a vast crowd. Crowds of mourners accompanied the coffins back through Mytholmroyd and Hebden Bridge. Sattonstall's gravestone now lies in Heptonstall church.

Food riots continued in Sheffield. In July 1795 Col Althorpe of the Volunteer Infantry lashed out with his sabre and ordered his soldiers to open fire. Two men were killed.

C L R

During the hungry 1840s Ebenezer Elliott (1781-1849) was wont to add the letters CLR (Corn Law Rhymer) after signing his name. One of eleven children, and son of a foundry owner, he was born at Masborough, near Rotherham, attended Penistone Grammar School and wed a wealthy young lady. By 1821 he was an ironmaster in Sheffield, retiring twenty-one years later.

But these were distressed times, and Ebenezer became a polemicist against the Corn Laws. Despite his own comfortable upbringing and success, he asked uncomfortable questions, such as:

'What is a Communist?
One who has yearnings
For equal division
Of unequal earnings.'

And a hymn:

'When wilt Thou save the people,
O God of Mercy, when?
The people, Lord, the people,
Not thrones and crowns, but men.'

He lampooned the idle rich in the image of 'Squire Leech'. His direct, sentimental poems, together with active Chartist and anti-corn law campaigns, served as an inspiration for the poor, and are part of his memorial. His statue stands in Weston Park, Western Bank, Sheffield.

COTTINGLEY FAIRIES

In the *Strand* magazine of Christmas 1920, Edward Gardner and Sir Arthur Conan Doyle were deceived into publishing an account of tiny fairies allegedly found in their Cottingley garden by two young girls, Elsie Wright and Frances Griffiths. A hoax, of course: the girls had made the images from cardboard, but for a time there were many believers.

COULD DO BETTER – AND DID

As the son of a grammar school headmaster, much was expected of young Alec Clegg. But with too many changes of maths teachers he lacked concentration, and after gaining only 10 per cent in school certificate maths, was nearly sent out as an apprenticed ironmonger. But after transferring to Bootham School, York, Alec re-took his exam, this time gaining 90 per cent. His success augured a great deal. He graduated with first-class honours as a linguist, taught for a while, and at the age of thirty-five became Director of Education for the West Riding of Yorkshire – a post he held with great distinction for the rest of his career. He died in 1986 at the age of seventy-seven.

COURTING

There have been many barriers to true love. In Victorian times at East Bierley a bar was fixed across the road to deflect non-residents, especially young men wishing to attract local girls.

And there were many variations of the Sunday p.m. 'monkey run'. Girls would walk up and down on one side of the street (e.g. Carlton Street, Castleford), boys on the other. These rituals, conducted in Sunday-best attire, might be dignified as 'parading', or in slightly posher areas (Bingley or Manningham Park, Bradford) as 'promenading'. When a couple went out together on several occasions, perhaps seeking a double seat at the rear of the cinema, they were said to be 'coppin' on', at first incurring a degree of teasing. In April 1921 the vicar of St Mary's, Horbury lamented young people's preferences: 'I think the parading up and down the streets which goes on in most towns on Sunday evenings and takes the place of churchgoing is a scandal and a disgrace to our country'. Finally, if you wanted the banns calling you were 'purrin in spurrins'.

CRAPPER, THOMAS (1836-1910)

Born near Thorne, Tom set up on his own after serving a plumbing apprenticeship. And no, he was not the inventor of the WC. This honour went to Joseph Bramah (born at Stainborough, 1748) who patented the first practical water toilet in 1778. Tom Crapper, though, carried the idea forward, increasing its popularity, inventing the ballcock and pioneering work in drainage and sanitation. Such was his reputation that he was given several Royal warrants, including the refurbishment of Sandringham House in the 1880s.

CRICKET CAPERS

Up to about 1939, when Wentworth Woodhouse was the home of the Fitzwilliams, much lively cricket was played on the lawn. A batsman heaving the ball into the house so as to break a window was awarded one pound, as well as six runs.

CRITICAL CLERIC

In his autobiography the Revd Francis Pigou, vicar of St John's Parish church, Halifax from 1875 until 1889, wrote of the 'high square pews in which it was whispered in my ear that rubbers of whist were sometimes played'. Moreover, the church was dilapidated, dusty, foul, the floor strewn with human remains, no better than a charnel house. During his incumbency the building was transformed.

CURIOUS CURES

For coughs and colds raspberry vinegar was a panacea, and generally liked by children; not so the brown paper covered in goose grease and hung around the chest. Camphor bags pinned to the vest helped breathing – though such youngsters couldn't hope to keep their plight from their classmates! Elderberry syrup was generally more popular than onion gruel. Some grandparents recommended mustard footbaths.

For a sore throat some elders advocated putting a roasted potato in a sock; mashing it till it steamed, then hanging it round the sufferer's neck.

Vinegar had many applications. One was to smear it over the forehead to ease a headache.

Against whooping cough, one school of thought recommended inhaling smoke in a train tunnel, as at Standedge.

Bairn with bronchitis, eh? Dig a hole, and place him in face down so he can breathe in near the fresh soil.

At Thornton in Edwardian times the knackers' yard owned by Messrs A. Bryant and Co. was opened to consumptives wishing to inhale gasses given off by breeding maggots.

Awkward splinter? Bandage the area with a sugar or soap poultice and leave overnight. Removal next morning should be easy.

At White Wells, Ilkley, gouty old men were doused in icy spring water.

Chilblains might be cured by applications from the overnight chamber pot.

During the 1920s a Honley herbalist, Norman Brookes, recommended clients try drinking their own urine.

A cure for diarrhoea was to sit over a chamber pot containing chamomile flowers boiled in milk.

A hot oven shelf wrapped in a blanket gave a bed warmth and comfort.

Around 1817 Dr John Taylor of Sheffield specialised in intestinal-worm treatments. His advertisements invited prospective patients to submit 'morning urine' samples. Herbal remedies were applied, resulting, occasionally, in fabulously long worms being evacuated.

Onions were another panacea, whether for rubbing on chilblains or resisting baldness.

CUTLERY – AND CUTTING EDGES

The industry had achieved national recognition in the time of Chaucer (1342-1400), for in the *Reeve's Tale* the Trumpington miller had a Sheffield 'thwitel' (dagger) in his hose. In 1540 John Leland reported of Sheffield, 'Ther be many smithes and cutelars in Hallamshire'. Inevitably the industry contributed to such saws as the following from Cobbler of Canterbury (*c.* 1590, and wisely anonymous): 'Women's wittes are like Sheffield knives, for they are sometimes so keene as they will cutte a haire, and sometimes so blunt that they must goe to the grindstone.'

No further comment – but think on!

DAFT TOFFEES

William Hardaker, generally known as Humbug Billy, kept a sweet stall in Green Market, Bradford. His peppermint supplier was Joe Neal, who (canny Yorkshireman that he was) was looking for summat cheaper than sugar. Trade substitutes, like powdered lime, were known as dafts. One purchase, though, in 1858, somehow contained arsenic – enough to make Hardaker himself badly ill after trying a toffee. Undaunted, he sold a few bags worth… after which twenty customers died, and scores were badly. Following the public outcry, laws were tightened on the adulteration of foods. Surprisingly, both Hardaker and Neal got off very lightly in this daft affair.

DEAN CLOUGH

The problem of what to do with redundant mills has been triumphantly solved with Dean Clough in Halifax. Once the biggest carpet mill in the world, it was two-thirds of a mile long; and by 1860 was the town's biggest employer with 5,000 workers. Closed in 1983 it has been reborn as a business park and an arts centre with theatre, art galleries and a hotel.

DEEPENING WATERS?

'Mixed bathing was allowed for the first time at the Lister Baths. There were over fifty couples present and Mr and Mrs Bilson saw that the Council's rules were strictly observed'. (*Pontefract and Castleford Express*, July 1912.)

DEEP HARMONY

This timeless hymn tune was written at the age of thirteen by Handel Parker (1854-1928) of Oxenhope, whose mother had been christened by Patrick Brontë. At seven he was playing the flute in the Drum and Fife Band; at fourteen he was church organist, and already working as a wool sorter. He taught flute, violin and trombone, becoming a brass band player, conductor and prolific hymn writer. But the work was not published until taken up by Duckworth of Colne in 1907.

Deep Harmony is associated with brass bands across Yorkshire – and beyond – and particularly with the Black Dyke Mills Band. Handel Parker was buried in Nab Wood Cemetery, Shipley, where the first few bars of *Deep Harmony* are set on his gravestone.

DENBY DALE PIES

The first pie was baked in 1788 to celebrate the return to sanity of King George III. The second was to celebrate the success of Waterloo (1815), when two sheep and twenty poultry were baked in a kiln. With the triumphant repeal of the Corn Laws (1846) the crowd may have become impatient at an over-long welcoming speech, for the pie was unceremoniously tumbled out of the cart (drawn by thirteen horses!). Nevertheless, the idea spread to Pudsey, where a huge 1,000lb pie was distributed among the poor.

With too many disparate ingredients (including mutton, pigeon, suet, turkey, and fox) the Great Jubilee Pie of 1887 went bad, and had to be buried in a wood. A more wholesome one was soon made. Next came the 1896 pie, marking the 50th anniversary of the repeal of the Corn Laws. The 1928 pie was a Huddersfield hospital fundraiser, dubbed 'Infirmary Pie'. The pie of 1964 was launched in the canal as a vessel to celebrate four royal births. It weighed six tons. It was eaten by 30,000 visitors. For the bicentenary pie, 1988, enjoyed by 70,000 eaters, 3,000 kilos of beef and potatoes and 700 kilos of onions were cooked in a huge dish, 18ft x 6ft, which has been retained as a flower bed by the town hall. Judging by the reception given to the AD 2000 Millennium Pie, future events will have to be mindful not only of public health concerns, but crowd control and parking.

DEVIL'S KNELL

All Saints church, Dewsbury, has several claims to fame. It is the only minster church in West Yorkshire. Patrick Brontë was a curate here for two years from 1809. Then there is the legend: a fifteenth-century lord of the manor, Sir Thomas de Soothill, murdered a servant boy, drowning him in a mill pond. To ward off further evil and to welcome Christ's birth with the hope of human redemption, he donated a bell to the church. Accordingly, every Christmas Eve the 13cwt Black Tom tenor bell is tolled slowly, one for every year AD. In order to ensure a prompt midnight finish a careful toll tally is kept.

DIALECT

Just one word can be so expressive. 'Wuthering', as in Emily Brontë's *Wuthering Heights*, means a strong, roaring, blustery wind. A 'polling' is a male haircut, possibly in

Denby Dale
pie dish.

someone's back kitchen. To 'scone' is to knock on the head with a fist (Castleford and district). 'Nesh' is fearful, reluctant, timid.
How about these:

Cow banging: transporting them
Sucked in: deceived, disappointed
Guttle: to eat ravenously, hurriedly, like glutton
Splatter-footed: knock-kneed
Keighley kay-legged 'uns: were rickety, owing to a poor diet

'Oile' needs a special mention: basically it means hole. Coil oile = coal hole. 'Penny oile' is a fine at the mill gate for latecomers who might complain, 'Ah were pennied'. Snap oile is an eating area. A three-oiler was a triple companionable set of earth closets (e.g. at Castleford, Pontefract), conjuring up memories of collective candle-lit visits. A picture oile was the cinema. And Bobby oile – yes, police station, of course!
Sayings:

'Tha talks an' says nowt.'
'Face like a bag o' spanners.'
'Green grocer were that stingy 'e'd nip a curran i' tew.'
'…wheer bods fly backards to keep muck out o' their een' (eyes)': could imply any industrial setting, like Pudsey, Cleckheaton, Batley.
''Im as taks religion ter mak brass'll 'appen find at finish he's gotten nowt i' God's bank.'
'If tha wants to lows (lose) a pal, lend 'im some brass.'
'Wakefill Libry? Ay, it's dahn theer, in't it, Alice, past them pubs? Grandowter hed to go theer for summat to do wi' 'er college.'

'Wom it!' Ah says to t' dog.'Ah'm that podged Ah canna shift!' (Go home, dog. I fear I have eaten too much…)

'Hard as nangnails,' which were corns, in the days of ill-fitting shoes.

'He were stood theer same as Joe Locke!' (A reference to the celebrated railway engineer whose statue stands in Locke Park, Barnsley, donated to the town by his wife in 1841. Joseph Locke was born in Attercliffe, 1805, his family moving to Barnsley five years later. He became a great pioneer, working first with George Stephenson on the Liverpool and Manchester Railway; then with Robert Stephenson and becoming chief engineer of the Grand Junction Railway, linking Birmingham with Liverpool and Manchester. He was elected a member of the Royal Society, 1830; and MP for Honiton, 1847. He died in 1860 and was buried in Kensal Green, London.)

It would be a major omission not to mention the phenomenal Joseph Wright, (1855-1930), 'an Idle man', as he said of himself… a donkey lad at six in a Windhill quarry, and a year later working as a half-time doffer at Saltaire woollen mill, taking full bobbins off the frames and replacing them. He remained illiterate until the age of fifteen, but becoming interested in the Franco-Prussian war, taught himself to read, attended night school, acquiring languages and science, even running a night school himself, charging a few pence per student.

In 1876, during short-time working at Baildon Bridge Mill, Joseph took himself off to Heidelberg where he studied German and maths. He served as a teacher in Bradford and further afield. Back he went to Heidelberg in 1882, specialising in languages and eventually gaining a PhD. After working in several universities he became Professor of Comparative Philology at Oxford, and compiler of the six-volume *English Dialect Dictionary, 1898–1905*, published at his own expense. Two million slips of paper would have put off many publishers! The Yorkshire Committee involved here became the nucleus of the Yorkshire Dialect Society in 1897, thought to be the world's oldest.

DOCK PUDDING FESTIVAL

Since 1971 the World Champion Dock Pudding Festival has been held in April or May at the Mytholmroyd Community Centre. Competitors bring pots of sweet docks (bistort), boiled with nettles, onions, oatmeal and fried with bacon or sausages. This unusual dish originated in nineteenth-century culinary experiments to feed the poor.

Sweet docks are reputedly good for relieving diarrhoea and other intestinal problems.

DONKEY WEDDING

'At last in August 1887, after much teasing, the cohabitees agreed to tie the knot at St Peter's church, Cleckheaton. The occasion, much publicised and well supported, brought a procession led by the town band, followed by twenty-eight donkeys and six more drawing the wedding coach. A reception at the Black Bull, Birstall ended with various entertainments including a bare-knuckle fight.'

Dore Well dressing (courtesy Anne Slater).

DONKEY LADS

Several West Yorkshire notables had connections, as boys, with donkeys. Joseph Wright is mentioned above. The philanthropic founder of Saltaire, Sir Titus Salt, as a schoolboy rode a donkey each day from the farm at Crofton to his lessons in Wakefield. An important third was Francis Chantrey (1781-1841) whose steed carried milk from a farm at Norton into Sheffield. Later he became a famous sculptor and painter.

DORE WELL DRESSING

Pre-Christian communities venerated water and its supposed deities; and like some other pagan customs, water symbolism was absorbed by the Christian church.

For West Yorkshire, the dressing of the wells is not really a Derbyshire import, as Dore was not a Derbyshire village until the county boundaries were redrawn in 1974. Since then, on the second Saturday in July, there has been a well display on the village green. A large wooden frame is spread over with soft clay, and the picture pricked out. Earlier, Biblical themes were favoured, but more recently secular ones have appeared. The scene is depicted using natural materials – flowers, petals, twigs, stalks, bark, evergreens, leaves, berries, seeds. It is a skilful art, and objects are designed to appear crisp and realistic.

Other wells have been dressed recently: St Mary's Well, Bridge End, Penistone, and in the Cragg Vale area.

DOUBLE-DECKER HOUSING

Hebden Bridge takes its name from the packhorse bridge over Hebden Water, which carried routes to Halifax, Burnley and Rochdale. Assisted by canal and railway, textile industries developed on the valley floor; indeed, this became 'trouser town'. To accommodate workers, tall terraced houses were built into the hillsides – four, even five storeys. The two storeys below opened onto a lower street. Stacked on top were two or more storeys, occupied by another family – plus any lodgers – with access from the hillside above.

DRINK

During the 1870s over 10 per cent of the Bradford police force was disciplined for drinking on duty. It was said that the quickest way out of Bradford was the beershop.

Brighouse was regularly cited for inebriated antics in late Victorian and Edwardian times. At Penistone the town crier, 'Pot-Oil' Ashton, quenched his thirst at the Rose and Crown, left behind his bell, memories and friends – and disappeared!

The Temperance movement, fostered by nonconformists, was aimed at abstinence. To this end the Band of Hope was founded by Jabez Tunnicliff in Leeds in 1847.

Chapels provided social alternatives, and working-class children, especially, were encouraged to sign the pledge. Shipley Glen set up a coffee house, and from the 1870s there were, for example, a British Temperance Tea and Coffee House at nearby Eldwick Green; and a Workmen's Coffee and Cocoa House at Rotherham. On Shrove Tuesday the Temperance Society held teetotal festivals in Brighouse town hall. A Women's Christian Temperance Union was formed in Ossett in 1891.

For anomaly lovers, what finer example of lateral Yorkshire thinking is there than to convert a temperance establishment into a pub? Situated next to the modern library is Keighley's former Temperance Hall, founded in 1896, but now the Livery Rooms, recalling an interim period when horses were stabled at the back.

DRUNKEN BARNABY

Ex-Royalist captain during the Civil War, Richard Braithwaite (1588-1673) came to write *Four Journeys to the North of England*, establishing himself as a social critic. He was, however, no paragon of virtue, being a scrounger, womaniser and tippler and holding magistrates and clergy in contempt. But there are interesting snippets of local colour in his accounts. He mentions industries like pin-making at Aberford, and that Tadcaster had 'a fair bridge, plenty of beggars and much broken pavement'. Here is an example of his scurrilous doggerel verse:

> Thence to Pomfrait; as long since is
> Fatall to our English Princes.
> For the choicest Licorice crowned
> And for sundry acts renowned;
> A louse in Pomfrait is not surer
> Than the Poor through sloth securer…

EARLY CO-OP

Meltham Mills, near Huddersfield, operated a Co-op from 1827, promoted by Jonas Brook on Shady Row, eighteen years before the Rochdale Pioneers.

EAST RIDDLESDEN HALL

James Murgatroyd, a flamboyant Halifax clothier, bought the Hall in 1638. But his ensuing debaucheries shocked neighbours and nature: it was claimed that the River Aire changed its course to avoid the estate. Within a generation, three family members were lodged in York Debtors' Prison. Several ghosts include a Grey Lady allegedly locked up to die for infidelity. The family may have inspired the Murgatroyd baronets in Gilbert and Sullivan's *Ruddigore*.

ECCLESIASTICAL ODDITIES

Amongst hundreds that might be listed is the following sample:

Lining a wall of the Chapel of St George in Sheffield Cathedral is a unique memorial screen of swords and bayonets of the York and Lancaster Regiment.

At St Peter's church, Thorpe Salvin (Rotherham) is a chained Bible – Bill's Bible of 1641, named after the printer Charles Bill of London.

An odd notice board dated 1735, situated behind the font in Fishlake church, lists standing orders above the name of James Pickman, 'Licens'd Clark'. Included are some lines concerning bellringers:

'And if any with Hatts on
Or Spurrs they do Ring
Four pence without grudging
Must pay unto Him.'

Old Tristram, standing a few feet behind the main south door of St John's parish church, Halifax, is an effigy modelled on a beggar from around 1700, whose pitch was around the church porch. He still collects from grateful visitors!

ECGBERT THE OVERLORD

On the village green at Dore stands a granite shield commemorating the success in AD 829 of King Ecgbert of Wessex in battle against Eanred of Northumbria, thus

Old Tristram, St John's Parish Church, Halifax.　　Overlord monument, Dore village green.

becoming overlord of all England. The result didn't last long: Ecgbert died in 839, and the Vikings continued their ravages. Still, it was a promising foretaste of what a future king of Wessex – Alfred – might do, even against the Danes.

ELECTION CELEBRATIONS, 1862

According to the *Wetherby News*, celebrations took an interesting turn in the Whitby Arms following the success of Sir John Ramsden and Sir Francis Crossley becoming MPs for the West Riding. All customers wearing hats had them burnt and ale was thrown down the steps into the street. Unnamed benefactors (the elected ones, or their agents, dare we guess?) bought more beer, and paid for replacement headgear from Ralph Whitehouse's shop in the market place.

ELECTORAL FIRST

Pontefract was first constituency to make use of the secret ballot in a by-election, 1872, the Right Hon Hugh Childers (Liberal) defeating Viscount Pollington (Tory). At this period ballot box seals showed imprints of Pontefract cakes! These boxes can be seen in the local museum.

ENOCH

Enoch Taylor is buried near the old stocks, opposite Marsden churchyard. He and his brother James were blacksmiths in Goodall's Yard, shoeing horses and improvising attachments for wagons and boats. But when they turned to making the first automatic shearing or cropping frames they prompted industrial unrest. The massive hammers which were used to smash the new frames were also dubbed 'Enoch'. Hence the croppers' (cloth finishers) rallying call against the threatened mechanisation of their industry: 'Enoch makes 'em and Enoch breaks 'em.'

Soon the Luddite campaign involved bloodshed. In April 1812 two Luddites were shot dead in the historic attack on Rawfolds Mill, Liversedge. Curiously, there were no hard feelings personally against the inventors – who were radicals and atheists anyway!

ENTREPRENEURS FROM NOWT

Michael Marks opened his penny bazaar in Kirkgate, Leeds in 1884. 'Don't ask the price – it's a penny,' was the invitation. Later he moved into the covered market. In 1894 he entered into partnership with Thomas Spencer of Skipton who put £300 into the scheme, Marks adding a further £450. They prospered. By 1924 Marks and Spencer Ltd had its headquarters in London.

In 1928 Harry Ramsden (1890-1963) started his fish and chip business in a wooden hut at White Cross, Guiseley. Take-away threepenny portions immediately became very popular with tram-terminus passengers. The venture proved such a winner that only three years later Harry opened the modern palatial restaurant. Always a stickler for detailed checks, he often swept up outside himself. There was no false modesty: he had a clock made with the hours marked by the letters of his name!

Enoch Taylor's grave, Marsden.

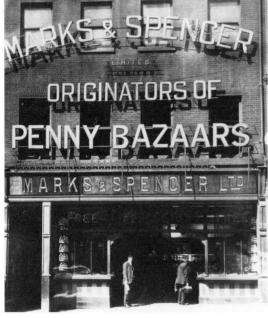

Penny Bazaar, Briggate, Leeds, 1909.
(Courtesy the Marks & Spencer Co.
Archive)

ENTREPRENEUR FROM SUMMAT

Col. John North (1842-96), born in Leeds, made a fortune in Chilean nitrates, gasworks and other industries. In his will he left Kirkstall Abbey to the City of Leeds for restoration and preservation.

EPITAPHS

Hezekiah Briggs, sexton and ringer, Bingley, who died in 1844, is remembered thus:

Here lies an old ringer beneath the cold clay
Who has rung many peals for serious and gay.
Bob majors and trebles with ease he could bang,
Till death called a 'bob' which brought the last clang.

And from Womersley, near Pontefract:

> Sacred to the Memory of George Hobman
> Blacksmith of Womersley, who departed
> this life April 17th 1851, aged 35 years.
> My Hammer and Anvil I've declined
> My Bellows they have lost their wind,
> My fire's extinct, my Forge decay'd
> And in the dust my Body's laid.

Catherine Alsopp, a Sheffield washerwoman found hanged in her bedroom on 7 August 1905, had scribbled her own epitaph, and with some forethought:

> Here lies a poor woman who always was tired;
> She lived in a house where help was not hired,
> Her last words on earth were, 'Dear friends, I am going
> Where washing ain't done, nor sweeping, nor sewing.
> But everything there is exact to my wishes,
> For where they don't eat, there's no washing of dishes.
> I'll be where loud anthems will always be ringing,
> But having no voice, I'll be clear of the singing.
> Don't mourn for me now, don't mourn for me never,
> I'm going to do nothing for ever and ever.

EVACUEES

Evacuees of the early days of the Second World War have become the stuff of folklore. During those first few weeks of September 1939 children from cities like Sheffield, Leeds and Bradford were widely dispersed to safer rural locations. Seventeen Leeds youngsters, for instance, were taken in by families at Scrooby, Nottinghamshire; but by Christmas many had returned.

In October two resourceful lads aged seven and nine, despatched to Leicestershire, managed to hitchhike back to Sheffield in one day!

FEATHER, TIM

Many communities claim a last weaver. Ossett's was George Nettleton, who died in 1907. Like many of his trade, George worked well into his eighties.

Baptised on 27 July 1825 by the Revd Patrick Brontë, Tim Feather became the legendary last handloom weaver. His loom, brought from a cottage bedroom at Buckley Green, Stanbury, near Haworth, is preserved in Cliffe Castle Museum, Keighley. A staple diet of porridge evidently served him well, as he was eighty-five years old when he died in 1910.

FEATHERSTONE MASSACRE

A century on, the 'massacre' legend lingers still. Various troubles had resulted in an employers' lock-out. The men were further aggrieved when coal was transported from Ackton Hall Colliery to Masham's Mill, Bradford; and on 7 September 1893 at Ackton Hall an angry crowd damaged windows and started fires. Unfortunately, police had been transferred to duty at the St Leger, Doncaster. Accordingly troops from the South Staffordshire Regiment were sent in. Their captain decided on a tactful withdrawal to the railway station. On their return the troops found a hostile assembly of some 2,000 men. A barrage of stones was followed by the reading of the Riot Act by Bernard Hartley, JP. The crowd failed to disperse. Warning shots fired in front of the crowd were thought to be blanks, but a second volley brought two deaths, those of James Gibbs and James Duggan; sixteen men were wounded. A long strike followed. At the inquest Duggan was ruled a 'justifiable homicide'; not so with Gibbs. Conflicting accounts were given to a Parliamentary commission. The bereaved families were awarded a hundred pounds.

The Home Secretary, Herbert Asquith (a Yorkshireman, born at Morley) was accused of brutality. A leaflet circulated bore on the cover, 'We would rather be shot down than hungered to death'. The affair remains a bitter folk memory.

FEMALE LABOUR

A gravestone in the Wesleyan Chapel graveyard at Luddenden Dean records the deaths in the 1890s of seven orphan girls, aged between twelve and seventeen, who worked at Calvert's Worsted Mill, Wainstalls. There is some mystery regarding the causes of these deaths. About this time some seventy young girls were brought from Kirkdale Industrial School, Liverpool to work in this mill.

FEUDAL LINKS

Tadcaster Court Rolls of 1550 show the lord of the manor's insistence on bakers pursuing their trade at his bakehouse – and paying their dues. In 1815 the *Leeds Intelligencer* warned people of the Old Mills area against grinding their own corn: evaders would be proceeded against. Here the custom was abolished in 1839. But at Horbury Soke Mill all corn had to be ground in the time-honoured way down to 1852.

'10th October 1756: Old Michaelmas Day and we turned our cattle into Huddersfield Town Ings, according to custom, and William Peaker had, with others, corn growing and our cattle eat it.' (*Day Books of John Turner*, 1732-1773.)

These were pre-enclosure times, with open fields and strip farming, so when the customary day arrived for communal grazing, individual strip holders left their crops unharvested at their own considerable risk.

FIRSTS

Robert Holgate (1481-1555), born at Hemsworth, was the first Protestant Archbishop of York and the first to be married. He founded in his native village a grammar school and a hospital for twenty poor men and women.

Yorkshire's first newspaper was the *Leeds Mercury* (1718), set up by John Hirst, the town's first known printer. In its early days it culled extracts from the London papers, but spread little local news.

Yorkshire's first balloon ascent was from Pontefract. In May 1785 James Sadler (1753-1828), already an experienced aeronautical pioneer, had drifted across from Manchester in windy conditions: he made a bad landing, and was injured when the balloon dragged him for two miles. Impressed by public sympathy, he decided to go up again from Pontefract.

Heckmondwike claims to be the first English town to have a public display of Christmas lights. The year was 1885. (Blackpool's September lights dated from 1879!)

The first Esperanto Society was formed in Keighley in 1902 by a journalist, Joseph Rhodes.

Betty Boothroyd, born at Dewsbury 1929, a former member of the Tiller Girl dancing troupe, was the first ever female Speaker of the House of Commons (1992-2000.) Despite abandoning the traditional Speaker's wig she kept the House in good order. After becoming a life peer, she went on to gain the Order of Merit (2005) and hold office as Chancellor of the Open University from 1994 to 2006.

FIRST FOOTING

Just after midnight, in the first minutes of the New Year, it had to be a male, dark-haired, who crossed the threshold carrying coal for warmth, bread for food, salt and a silver coin for good fortune.

FISHY ADVERT

During the later Victorian decades certain Skipton traders caught the fashion of advertising their wares in verse. One example went:

> This is to let the people know
> When they want fish where they can go
> And buy some nice, fresh and sweet
> At W. Hogg's, No. 91 High Street.

Hogg was a Skipton fishmonger and poet of the 1880s.

FIVE RISE LOCKS

The opening of John Longbotham's superb engineering feat at Bingley on 21 March 1774 attracted some 30,000 spectators. Five locks, each holding nearly 90,000 gallons of water, were linked like a staircase to overcome the challenging gradient, lifting boats 60ft over 350 yards! The completion of this section of the Leeds-Liverpool Canal, the longest in Britain (127 miles) helped the industrialisation of the Aire Valley substantially.

FLOATING LING

Fiddler, soldier, carrier, road builder: despite his handicap, Blind Jack Metcalf of Knaresborough (1717-1810) was a highly skilled man of many professions.

Commissioned by a turnpike trust to build a road connecting Wakefield, Huddersfield and Saddleworth, he had to find a way over some difficult marshy terrain at Standedge Common. Believing in good drainage, with convex surfaces to drain away rainwater, and realising that stone tended to sink, he designed as a foundation a series of rafts from ling – bundles of rushes, marsh grass and heather. He was ridiculed at first but the idea worked. Altogether Blind Jack built 180 miles of road. The principle was copied by George Stephenson in laying the Manchester-Liverpool railway over Chat Moss.

FLOODS

In mid-afternoon of 18 May 1722, after a cloudburst, the waters of the River Ryburn rose and lives were lost. 'Ripponden Chapel was much damaged, part of the churchyard washed away, the graves laid open, and a coffin was lodged in a tree at a considerable distance'. (*Annals of Yorkshire*, Vol. I, Parson and White.) The church was rebuilt on higher ground.

St Mary's church, Tadcaster has known fire and flood. The Scots burnt it down in 1318 during one of their periodic incursions. Rebuilt, it was often invaded by the flooding of the too-adjacent River Wharfe. Between 1875 and 1877 the stones of the

Five Rise Locks, Bingley.

T'Owd Genn, Towngate, Holmfirth.

nave were painstakingly taken down and again rebuilt, this time with raised foundations of 5ft connecting to the untouched tower.

Holmfirth had known earlier floods in 1738 and 1777, but nothing like that of 5 February 1852, when just after midnight the Bilberry Reservoir burst through its dam. Eighty-one people were drowned, and livestock, homes, mills and bridges were destroyed. On Towngate the Owd Genn Memorial (a gritstone pillar by the normally quiet River Holme, and named after its sculptor, Henry Genn) shows that floodwaters reached, astonishingly, some 7ft above ground level. The church opposite was flooded to a level of 5ft. In St David's church, Holmbridge, which was inundated, there is a Bible whose pages are imprinted with steel-rimmed spectacles owned by a Mrs Hirst. She clapped the book shut when the flood alarm was raised and escaped in time. Uprooted coffins were found among the pews, together with a drowned goat. An inquest severely criticised the Commissioners of the Holme reservoirs for the faulty construction of the dam in the previous decade.

FOLKLORE

'Bradford for cash,
Halifax for dash,
Wakefield for pride and poverty.
Huddersfield for show,
Sheffield, what's low,
Leeds for dirt and vulgarity.'

FONT RUSH

With the Births, Marriages and Deaths Registration Act coming into effect on 1 July 1837 there were widespread fears that baptismal fees would rise. Consequently, many hitherto laggardly families hastened to make appointments with their parson. Huddersfield recorded eighty-six baptisms in one day; Leeds and Bradford had over four hundred each.

FOOD

Parkin (or pepper cake) is a tasty blend of oatmeal, carroway seeds, treacle, ginger and a touch of pepper (with pig's blood, according to some older connoisseurs). It is generally prepared in late October for All Saints Sunday and Bonfire Night, with another batch made ready for Christmas.

How to feed a family in hard times? That was the question. Tripe shops did well in industrial towns; some families ate it cold with vinegar, bread and butter. A good winter standby was sheep's head broth. Butchers generally gave them away, and pigs' heads too, but charged a copper or two for trotters and cow heel. When money was tight, or just before pay day, the menu might be reduced to Resurrection Pie – potatoes with odd scraps of meat or such vegetables as could be obtained. Hungry Gaps might be filled with nettle soup, boiled up with butter, flour, milk, seasoning and owt left ower!

Frumenty (Latin *frumentum*, corn) was made from pearled wheat, soaked and boiled up with milk, water, sugar, cinamon, rum or spirits. Traditionally it was a Christmas treat.

At summer tea-times during the 1920s and 1930s children would often be seen in the street nibbling a tea cake, a slice of fruit loaf, or bread smeared with lard, dripping – or even condensed milk and cocoa!

The toasting fork is now a museum piece. But there was nowt better than to cap a thick slice o' toast, pushed against a glowing Sunday tea-time coal fire, and then spread over with beef dripping and lightly salted.

Started in 1984, the Pork Pie Appreciation Society meets every Saturday evening in the Old Bridge Inn, Ripponden.

Funeral feasts are prominent in Yorkshire folklore – 'See 'em off with ham,' was one dictum. But there were variations – indeed, few boundaries – and even a moderate list might also include plum cake and cheese, parkin, apple pie and ale.

FOOTBALL CLUB AUCTIONED

Leeds City Football Club was formed in 1904 and entered the football league in the following year. As such they were the city's leading professional club for many years. But owing to financial irregularities the club was expelled, and the sixteen players were auctioned off, for a total of £9,250, to nine other clubs at the Metropole Hotel on 17 October 1919.

Leeds United was soon formed, entering the league in 1920.

FOOTBALL FROM CRICKET

It is curious that a number of league soccer teams originated from cricket clubs. Sheffield Wednesday (the Owls, 1867) began with Sheffield Wednesday Cricket Club which had started in 1820, Wednesday being a favoured day by Little Mesters (*see* LM). Sheffield United (the Blades, 1889) was an offshoot of the Yorkshire County Cricket Club which played at Bramall Lane from 1855.

FRIDAY FETTLING

There were many jobs to be done about the house on Fridays. For a start, once the men and bairns had left, the coal-fired range, boiler, oven, the lot had to be black-leaded – and, for the house-proud, done over with methylated spirits to bring up the shine.

Then there was donkey stoning of the front door step, aye – and any flag stones up to the coursey (pavement) were a matter of decorative pride, to be scrubbed every Friday morning, with many a sideways glance at how neighbours were progressing along the terrace. Cleanliness without betokened good order within. Donkey stones were so-called because this animal was the brand image of an early manufacturer of a favourite cream, brown or white soap.

FRUGALITY

Being careful with money was apt to be born of family custom. Industrial Yorkshire has known long periods of unemployment, dole queues, sickness and misfortune. The eldest of nine children, John Carr (1723-1807), architect of Harewood House, York Assize Courts, Wakefield House of Correction etc knew poverty as a boy in Horbury. There were times when he had to stay in bed while his trousers were mended.

In his famous work *Self Help*, which appeared in 1859, Samuel Smiles (1812-1905) preached frugality and self-sufficiency, with many examples of how deprived people had improved their lot. For twenty years from 1838, this former doctor edited the *Leeds Times*, founding a Temperance Hall and Mechanics Institute in Woodhouse.

Hard times were apt to breed stoicism and a blunt laconic attitude. But there were many occasions when cynicism turned to a more sinister kind of self-help. When in November 1799 Huddersfield soup kitchens raised charges to a penny a quart, some customers took to stealing corn from warehouses.

In general, however, cheapness with reasonable quality was sought, and often found, in the local Co-op, where the declaration of seasonal 'divi' (dividend, so much back in the pound) was a red letter day. Stories are told of times when rent days involved a furtive fifteen hour look-out from the vantage point of an upstairs window. We may laugh now at such accounts, and at the Poverty Grace:

O Heavenly Father, bless us
And keep us all alive;
There's ten of us for dinner
And food for only five.

But for many people 'just getting by' was a serious business.

FULNECK: THE MORAVIAN SETTLEMENT

Situated on the rural edge of Pudsey, this Moravian village from the 1740s is a social and cultural enclave with distinctive chapel, school, workshops and social clubs. The exquisite Georgian terrace is the longest in Britain of its period. The inspiration for the settlement came from an Ossett clergyman, Benjamin Ingham, a friend of the Wesleys, who found his evangelical work better suited to fields and barns than Anglican

Georgian terrace, Fulneck.

churches. His Moravian friends were sympathetic, and with due initiative set up a new community at Fulneck. The name derives from 'Fulnek' in Northern Moravia (now the Czech Republic), from where the early settlers came. Their ancestors have some claim to be the first Protestant Church, separating from Roman Catholicism back in 1457. A more recent claim is to house England's only Moravian museum – and with the oldest working fire engine, c. 1825.

GARTER IMPROVISATION

About 1835 Charles Revitt famously mended the bellows that worked Dore church's harmonium with the garter of a lady chorister.

GIBBETED

The notorious highwayman Spence Broughton (1746-1792), put on trial for robbing the Sheffield-Rotherham mail, was executed at York on 14 April 1792. On the scaffold he appeared contrite and asked for prayers for his soul. Two days later his corpse was put into a gibbet – an iron frame – and hung up on Attercliffe Common near the scene of his crime (as was the gibbeting tradition). It was estimated that 40,000 sightseers visited the scene that first day. Subsequently the rotting body was looked on with awe by countless thousands, remaining on public view until 1827.

Road travel was still hazardous at this time. It is startling to find in 1830 the Wakefield town crier urging butchers and dealers to travel home from the cattle market in bands of at least ten, in the hope of putting off highwaymen.

GRAVE SITUATIONS

A beer barrel monument to a local boozer is to be found in St John's churchyard, Kirkheaton. Was this the widow's revenge? Much more serious is the monument to seventeen children killed by fire in 1818.

In Kildwick St Andrew's churchyard an organ monument was raised to John Laycock, organ maker, who died 13 September 1889, aged eighty-one.

Suicides were sometimes buried at crossroads. Richard Commons, after some bacchanalian festivity, set his house alight in 1623 and hanged himself in the midst of the blaze. He was buried at crossroads to the north of Halifax.

There is a gravestone to a pet gander, Dick (1900-1923), at Triangle (near Sowerby Bridge) on a grass verge along the Manchester-Halifax road.

John Logan, at rest in Halifax parish churchyard, died in 1830 at the age of 105, after being twice wed, and fathering thirty-two children.

Opened in 1852, Undercliffe Cemetery on the Otley Road, Bradford accommodates monuments and obelisks, displaying opulent grandeur even in death for notables and the well-to-do. Lister Lane Cemetery, Halifax, opened 1841 has similar memorials.

By contrast, at the other end of the social scale were such outlooks as 'Our Gladys isna goin' to last long. Ah've just 'ad closet seat mended for t' funeral.'

Sheffield inn with memorabilia of highwayman Spence Broughton.

Grave of John Laycock, organ builder.

GREATCOATS FOR THE ENEMY

It has been claimed that a million greatcoats made in West Yorkshire factories found their way through Napoleon's embargo and onto the backs of French soldiers for the invasion of Russia in 1812.

GRETNA GREEN OF THE WEST RIDING

Parson Taylor, curate-in-charge (1755-1793) at Rothwell parish church, was the subject of local gossip. One likely topic was the number of irregular runaway marriages he conducted.

WILLIAM GRIMSHAW

Many anecdotes have been told of this fire and brimstone parson, incumbent at Haworth from 1743 to 1762 following ministries at nearby Littleborough and Todmorden. Not only were non-attenders browbeaten on their own doorstep: as a muscular Christian he used strong-arm methods to bring backsliders into church from the adjacent Black Bull. Interestingly, he had been a drinker and a reveller himself as a young man. Sometimes he asked a warden to read a long psalm while he went looking to increase his congregation. He aimed at good order and the suppression of vice, and became an admired, if an exceptionally authoritarian figure. Rival Sabbath pursuits like football were suppressed, and Divine Aid sought against horse races and attendant evils. His prayers were followed by three days of rain, and the unseemly races never resumed.

Despite some very long sermons his congregations overflowed into the churchyard. Communicants increased from a dozen to 1,200. He was generous to visitors and travelling preachers, particularly his Methodist brethren. John Wesley paid many visits, preaching to huge congregations. Critics called him Mad Grim, but for supporters he was dubbed the Apostle of Yorkshire.

Another strong-arm vicar was the Revd Bellas of Marsden (1779-1815), a fighter who, it was said, knocked religion into parishioners. Reputedly, however, he had 'more ale in him than religion.'

JOHN GULLY (1783-1863)

To be able to buy Ackworth Park meant serious money. John Gully had it, made through shrewd gambling, a knowledge of horseflesh and some toughening worldly experiences. Imprisoned for debt when his butcher's business, near Bath, failed, but known as a bare-knuckle fighter, he was befriended by Henry Pearce,

William Grimshaw of Haworth.

the redoubtable champion 'Game Chicken'. Eventually they fought over sixty-four rounds, and the young challenger had to give in. But when Pearce shortly retired, John Gully was his acknowledged successor. Taking on a London pub, he acquired contacts and began attending race meetings, including Doncaster. Turf accountancy was the next step; falling out with his partner, he horsewhipped him and then paid him £500 for the pleasure.

Now a rich man, Gully invested money in coal, bought Ackworth Park, and in 1832 paid his way into winning the Parliamentary seat for Pontefract, holding it for five years. He was presented at court in 1836. On returning to racing he enjoyed huge successes, his steeds winning the Derby three times, and in 1854 the Two Thousand Guineas as well.

A punning doggerel verse by James Smith is worth quoting:

> You ask me the cause that made Pontefract sully
> Her fame, by returning to Parliament Gully?
> The etymological cause I suppose is –
> His breaking the bridges of so many noses.

Most of us will need reminding that the name 'Pontefract' derived from 'broken bridge'. Gully married twice, fathering twenty-four children.

On 14 March 1863 he was buried against the church wall at Ackworth in his own grounds.

HALF-TIMERS

Limited schooling was to be provided for working children by an Act of 1844. Often in lessons they were weary and idle. In 1873, ten-year-old Ben Turner, born in Austonley, near Huddersfield, worked in a woollen mill, on an alternating routine. The first week he worked in the mill from 6 a.m. to 12.30 p.m., and spent two and a half hours in school during the afternoon; during the second week morning school was followed by four and a half hours in the mill. Either way he was very tired, which made for inattention, and for many breaches of school discipline.

In 1913 there were more than 19,000 half-timers in the West Riding, nearly half of them in Bradford. The pernicious system lingered until 1922.

HALIFAX GIBBET

Between 1541 and 1650, forty-two men and six females were guillotined in this town. On 9 January 1572 alone there were three victims. This awesome sanction was imposed especially for the theft of goods valued at thirteen and a half pence or more. Lesser offenders might be nailed by the ear to the gibbet post and given a knife to get free – all of which made for the entertainment of the crowd. One thief, John Lacy, somehow escaped at the last moment, but unwisely returned to the town seven years later – and

this time the axe fell on his neck. The last felon had stolen sixteen yards of kersey cloth drying on tenterframes.

No wonder the prayer went up: 'From Hell, Hull and Halifax, Good Lord, deliver us.' Hull, too, imposed severe penalties; its jail was unpleasant, even by the standards of the day.

The gibbet's original blade is preserved at the Bankfield Museum.

HAVERCAKES

Special mention must be made of this favourite Yorkshire dish. Havercakes ingredients were oatmeal, water, butter, salt, milk and yeast, thoroughly mixed and cooked on bakestones – oblong iron sheets – over a slow fire. After being hung up to dry the oatcakes resembled wash leathers. They could be eaten as a savoury dish – say, cheese or bacon – or with treacle, like pancakes. They were popular in some stores up to the 1950s.

The badge of the 33rd Regiment of Foot, the Duke of Wellington's, was an oatcake, and these soldiers were renowned as the Havercake Lads (Scandinavian *hafri* were oats). In the hope of attracting hungry volunteers, a recruiting sergeant would flourish a pierced havercake on the end of his sword. The Cutlers Company of Sheffield sometimes ate brewis, a kind of soup sprinkled with oatcake, in recognition of the staple diet of earlier generations of apprentices.

One wonders why Havercake Ale was so long in arriving: with the tercentenary in 2002 of the Duke of Wellington's Regiment (now the Third Battalion of the Yorkshire Regiment) it did.

HAWORTH HEALTH, 1850

Responding to complaints made by the Revd Patrick Brontë, Benjamin Babbage included in his *Report for the General Board of Health* in London such details as an open sewage channel down Main Street, and privvies amounting to sixty-nine for 2,500 people (although the parsonage had a two-seater). One cellar dwelling housed a family of seven who slept in two beds. Average life expectancy in the village was twenty-five years. Forty-one per cent of infants died before they were six.

Babbage might have added that it was no wonder the Brontë girls preferred to stretch their legs on the moors above! Top Withens, the farmhouse ruin on the moor, is thought to be one of the inspirations for Emily's *Wuthering Heights*.

HENPECK'D CLUB

It's difficult to get at facts – mainly because some husbands have been secretive. In 1862 Harry Tap (real name Henry Hargreaves Thompson) drew up a rule book for his members meeting furtively at his Royal Oak Inn, Keighley, showing how husbands might cherish their wives by such kindly acts as cleaning their shoes, doing errands uncomplainingly and getting their own supper. *Taming the Shrew* was a sub-title, or *The New Method*.

Thus the question must arise – are we in the realms of tongue-in-cheek male propaganda, drawn up over a half-pint or two? Well, yes. And ample confirmation is available in that practical joke displayed in Keighley's Cliffe Castle Museum: a wife-taming cradle in which a nagging woman could (theoretically, of course) be placed and rocked by Club members until she had become more amenable. A selfish yet emotionally satisfying masculine thought…

The Club disbanded when Harry got wed. Whether other clubs were later formed in the Cragg Vale/Halifax districts, and, indeed, whether husbands over a wider Pennine area still foregather in secret rendezvous to escape their ladies for an hour or two cannot be revealed here.

HEPTONSTALL

This is an exceptional hilltop village, reached by a slow climb out of Hebden Bridge, with spectacular views over the Calder and Colden Valleys. The gritstone cottages in Weavers Square once housed handlooms; there was no water power, as at Hebden Bridge, up here. The Square provides the venue for the Pace Egging play on Good Friday.

Immediately below, the graveyard has that rare claim – two churches. St Thomas the Apostle was built in 1854 to replace the medieval church, dedicated to St Thomas a Beckett, which was ruinously damaged in a storm in 1847. Famous graves include those of David Hartley, the notorious 'King of the Cragg Vale Coiners', hanged at York in 1770. Sylvia Plath (1932-1963), poet and wife of former Laureate Ted Hughes was also laid to rest here.

The Cloth Hall, built in around 1550 and hence the oldest in Yorkshire, was built by the Waterhouse family of Shibden Hall. Handloom weavers brought their cloth here for sale to middlemen. Trade declined during the early eighteenth century because the wares were increasingly taken into Halifax.

The Grammar School was endowed in 1642, rebuilt in 1771, and remained in use until 1889. It is now a museum with various scholastic artefacts as well as coining equipment.

The Mechanics' Institution, founded in 1868, served as a social club and reading room, offering lectures for ordinary working men.

The foundation stone of the octagonal Methodist chapel was laid by John Wesley in 1764. He had asked for this special building so that all parts of the congregation could, hopefully, see and hear the preacher. (Locals may also tell you that an octagonal building has no corners for the Devil to hide!) But when roofing seemed beyond the capabilities of local builders, Wesley had it made in Rotherham and transported in

Two churches in Heptonstall churchyard.

Quaker stone, Heptonstall.

sections by horse and cart. Reputedly he visited the village sixteen times. The chapel is the oldest still in use.

Among many historical claims to fame is the fact that in 1643 the village was a Parliamentary garrison besieged by Royalists (*see* Civil War). Reminders of former times include a windowless dungeon, stocks, pump and pinfold. And amid wooded Hardcastle Crags is Gibson's Mill, a nineteenth-century cotton mill. By 1902, being no longer competitive, it closed down and was converted into an entertainments centre with dance hall, roller-skating rink and dining saloon. Never a satanic mill, Gibson's has been renovated by the National Trust and is open to visitors.

According to an uncomplimentary ditty:

Halifax is built o' wax,
Heptonstall o' stone;
Halifax has bonny lasses
Heptonstall's got none!

HERMIT OF RUMBALD'S MOOR

As a boy, Job Senior (*c.* 1785-1857) was brought up near Ilkley, working intermittently at woolcombing and drystone walling. Despite a drink problem, he proved to be a remarkable singer and was engaged by several town theatres. At the age of sixty he wed in Otley church a widow in her eighties, Mary Barrett, with a calculated eye on her smallholding near Burley Woodhead. Job squandered her money, not caring for her too well, and as he had expected she soon died. But Nemesis took a hand when her disgruntled relatives ransacked the home. Woeful and desperate, Job built a rough shelter, little more than a kennel, from the debris. For years he survived, unkempt, in a straw-packed coat, despite some arson attempts on his hovel. For curious sightseers with ready money he sang, told fortunes and forecast the weather – a move which gained credulity when in advance of a bad storm he tied down his roof while others mocked. He also offered marriage guidance (but, perhaps understandably, his counsel was mostly negative). Latterly he suffered from rheumatism and leaned heavily on two sticks. He was reduced to living on potatoes and beer. After his ale was poisoned, Job became ill, spending his last days in Carlton workhouse. He was buried at Burley in Wharfedale. There is a reminder in a local pub, The Hermit at Burley Woodhead.

HINDENBERG OVER KEIGHLEY

On 23 May 1936 the German airship *Hindenberg* dropped a crucifix and a bunch of carnations over Keighley. An accompanying letter from a priest, John Schulte, requested that they should be placed on the grave of his brother, who had died in a Skipton prisoner-of-war hospital. And so it was done. This apparent errand of mercy, however, was one of many unscheduled flights made by German airships over Yorkshire at this time; it is likely that the increasingly menacing regime of Adolf Hitler may have been doing reconnaissance with a view to future plans for the area.

HIRING FAIRS

They began with the Statute of Labourers, 1351, which aimed at stabilising the supply of labour after the ravages of the Black Death. The resulting annual sittings or 'statis' were fixed for prescribed days and places, with due regard for local conditions and wage trends. Accordingly, hirings became a feature of life in market towns and larger villages. November (Martinmas, or locally, 'Martlemas') was a favoured season, with most routine farm work completed in many places like Rotherham and Doncaster, though there was considerable variation. The Kippax 'Statice' took place at the end of October, and Sheffield's on the feast of St Simon and St Jude, 28 October. But St John's Tide Fair, Halifax, was held at the Feast of John the Baptist on the 24 June.

Farm servants seeking new jobs put themselves up for hire in the market place, and customarily wore a badge advertising their calling; a shepherd, for example, displayed a tuft of wool in his lapel. A girl looking for kitchen work might wear a wooden spoon in her apron string. Most appeared in their Sunday best. By the later nineteenth century young women had been prudently moved indoors – at Wetherby inside the town hall.

A token sum – the 'fastening penny' – was given by the prospective employer to clinch the bargain. The sum would depend on the hired person's experience and new rank. An experienced waggoner would expect and receive more than a young lad fresh from school. Such direct wage bargaining was an excellent example of the forces of supply and demand working over the centuries.

Young men lived in on the farm. Horse lads, in particular, were part of a fine tradition, taking great pride in their horses, even stealing titbits for them. Married men moved into tied cottages.

Gradually, and increasingly during the nineteenth century, the hirings became fairs, with roundabouts, punch-and-judy stalls, menageries, quack doctors, freaks, steam horses, wild-beast shows etc. At Cleckheaton a trombonist lured folk to see a tooth-puller operating from a coal merchant's cart, with loud music drowning any screams. Old friends were re-united. Servants exchanged gossip *re* past employers. Pubs were busy and noise flared sometimes into violence. The hirings provided the opportunity to settle old scores. The Doncaster hirings of 1868 was memorably described by C. W. Hatfield as the biggest babel of dialects since Noah!

Inevitably, and no doubt rightly, the statute fairs incurred much criticism from clergy and others. In a speech at Bradford Lord Brougham condemned them, claiming they were too often designed 'for the purpose of promoting intemperance'. School attendance was seriously affected; many simply granted holidays.

The Leeds hirings faded out in the 1860s; Wakefield's by the turn of the century. Some, like Wetherby's and Doncaster's, lasted into the twentieth century, until labour exchanges, newspaper advertisements and the Agricultural Wages Act of 1924 made them redundant.

HOME ON T' RANGE

Time was when the ubiquitous cast-iron fireplace burning wood, coal or peat was the only source of heating. Kettles were boiled on it, and meat was cooked in an inbuilt oven. Some ranges were fitted with a reckon hook so the saucepan could be moved inwards over the fire. The boiler had to be topped up from well or spring. The mantlepiece was likely to be a miscellany of bric-a-brac including pot dogs, candlesticks, clay pipes and sepia photographs. Boots and clogs dried on the hearth. Covering parts of the flagstone floor were peg rugs with cut-up cloth strands interwoven on a patterned hessian base.

An interesting range has been preserved in the Colne Valley Museum at Golcar.

HONEST DODWORTH

It was late at night and the pubs had shut. One reveller, for a bet, shinned up a lamp post and placed an allegedly gold watch on top: it seemed a good idea at the time. Next morning, seeking a time check, his memory slowly returned. Drawing on his clothes, he hastened along the street… and found that his watch was still there. 'Honest Dodworth!' he shouted, surprised and greatly relieved. Locals like to think that theirs is still a community of integrity.

HORSE TRAFFIC

Until steam power and the internal combustion engine, horses were the norm. Our streets were populated by farm carts, milk men, greengrocers, fire engines… as an older generation will remember. Doctors and parsons rode in light gigs or traps, or even on horseback. Village carriers came into town with goods and gossip, giving rise to numerous tales of steeds knowing their way from one hostelry to another. Eventually public transport was harnessed. In 1858 Leeds had a horse bus service calling at Headingly and Roundhay. From 1873 Sheffield had horse-drawn trams, running on steel rails, with lines to Attercliffe, Brightside and Heeley. The horses were picturesque, and though not presenting intolerable parking problems they were not pollution-free: regular accumulations of horse manure made pedestrians watchful and wary.

HOTTS FOR BATLEY

Early eighteenth-century 'hotts' were boxes which hung like panniers on the horses which carried manure to fields around small towns like Batley and Dewsbury. They were opened underneath and the contents scattered. It tended to be women's work, though the heavier muck pluggin' – laborious spreading over broader acres – was done by men.

HUDDERSFIELD CHORAL SOCIETY

It all began on the 7 June 1836 with a meeting at the Plough Inn, Westgate. The founder members were sixteen musicians, teetotallers from chapels and churches. Women choristers were also welcomed. Soon monthly meetings were held on Friday evenings at an infants' school on Spring Street, moonlight helping distant singers to walk safely. There were some strict regulations. While perquisites allowed three gills of ale, with bread and cheese, members were fined 3d if they were late for rehearsals. Another rule stipulated that 'no person shall be a member who frequents the Hall of Science or any of the Socialist meetings'. From the start much sacred music was promoted, with Handel very popular (above all his *Messiah*).

With the opening of the town hall in 1881 concerts began to feature the celebrated Charles Halle and his orchestra. Internationally distinguished conductors of a later period included Sir Malcolm Sargent (1932-67).

The Halifax Choral Society claims to be older, however, having started in 1817!

HUDDERSFIELD RAILWAY STATION

This beguilingly elegant classical portico, with eight Corinthian columns, was designed in 1847 by James Pritchett of York. It has been highly praised by numerous connoisseurs of urban architecture. John Betjeman labelled it England's 'most splendid station façade'.

Huddersfield railway station.

Flanked by colonnaded wings formerly at odds with much local industrial building, the station stands supreme in a fine uncluttered square.

✦ ୧ ✦

IF

Some 'ifs' are remote and fanciful speculations. Others can be seen as near misses. For example:

If only Fred Trueman (1931-2007), champion fast bowler, who gave no quarter and asked for none, had been born a few hundred yards to the south he would have played for Notts. As it was he was born at Stainton, and was the first cricketer to take 300 Test wickets. It's hard to imagine him weeping, emotionally overcome, in the dressing room afterwards. Fred's international tally was 307 wickets in only 67 matches, at a cost of only 21.57 runs. He retired at thirty-seven – very late even for this bluff, downright, great-hearted Yorkshireman.

Then there were the Priestleys. Drink has ruined many a man, but not Birstall-born Joseph Priestley (1733-1804). After various travels he became in 1767 a popular Presbyterian minister at Mill Hill Chapel, Leeds, living in a house next door to the Meadow Lane brewery. He made a few tentative visits… to study fermentation. He found that a lighted candle lowered into a partially filled tank went out on reaching the carbon dioxide layer. This led him to further experiments with gases, and he successfully isolated oxygen. Taking up chemistry he became a distinguished scientist

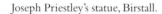
Joseph Priestley's statue, Birstall.

and a Fellow of the Royal Society. He very nearly went as astronomer on Captain Cook's second voyage – and therein lies another 'if'... What might he have achieved there?

As well as being one of science's immortals, Joseph was a controversial man of the cloth. His *History of the Corruptions of Christianity* was burnt by the public hangman on the Continent. He contributed to the wording of the American Constitution and helped to set up Leeds Library.

But what if, as many fellow clergy urged congregations from their pulpits, he had gone nowhere near drink?

J.B. Priestley sometimes helped his headmaster father Jonathon with classes at Green Lane School, Bradford. He was a lively young man, loved by the children. He even got one class to describe the head (who was a martinet, quick-tempered and inclined to cane first and ask questions later). What an inspirational teacher John Boynton would have made – but what a loss to literature.

And what if, in 1727, John Wesley's application for the headmastership of Ermysted Grammar School, Skipton had not been turned down? He was not alone in seeing such posts as sources of income. These were days of bribery and bad behaviour – not all of it by the boys. We can only speculate how things might have turned out. Would his religious mission have been replaced by comparable educational fervour?

ILLEGITIMACY

The 1662 Act of Settlement aimed to return single women found to be pregnant and likely to become an additional charge on the poor rate to their native parishes. Such was the fate of Elizabeth Taylor, removed from Dore to Manchester in 1826, to be provided for by that town's Overseers of the Poor. Conceptions on the 'wrong side o' blanket' continued to be a stigma until our own times.

ILLITERACY

To this day full adult working literacy has still not been achieved. In the pre-schools era, many a couple at their wedding simply 'made their mark'. Despite Lord Hardwicke's Marriage Act of 1754 requiring both bride and groom to sign the church register, not all couples could do so. At Sprotbrough in the second half of the eighteenth century half the grooms were sufficiently literate, but only a quarter of the brides. Of twenty-six weddings during the decade 1754-64, there were only five where both partners signed.

There were many misgivings about the teaching profession, such as it was. Dr Alfred Gatty, vicar of Ecclesfield from 1839 to 1903, claimed that Rawson's Infants School was run by an old woman who signed her name with a cross when paid her quarterly salary.

INDUSTRIAL REVOLUTION FORERUNNERS

From medieval times many villages like Marsden, Heptonstall and Thurlstone were established as textile centres.

Sheffield was already known for sickles, shears etc in the fourteenth century. Chaucer's Miller in the *Canterbury Tales* carried a thwitel (knife) in his hose. In the Chapter House of Sheffield Cathedral a window is devoted to scenes and characters from the *Tales*. The town's cutlers were incorporated in 1624. Independent smithies proliferated in neighbouring villages. Watermills were recorded as early as the twelfth century.

Kirkstall Abbey had a forge and developed such industries as copper, lead, tanning, pottery, spinning and weaving; lay brothers worked another forge at Ardsley and a coal mine at Cookridge. These Cistercian monks learned by observation and digging that coal deposits were often found beneath a layer of clay on which large-leaved clovers flourished. Iron ore was worked at Tankersley, Dodworth and Wortley. It is clear that monastic enterprise over a wide area bequeathed a handy industrial base to the later economic life of Leeds. (See other matters under Kirkstall Abbey.)

Armley Mills, Leeds (using water power for the fulling process) was set up in mid-sixteenth century by clothier Richard Booth. It was to become the world's largest woollen mill, working until 1969; since then it has served as an industrial museum.

There were important developments in the glass industry. From 1658 Pot House Hamlet, Silkstone had the first glassworks in Europe, with coal-fired furnaces for both green and white glass, although it petered out over the next century. At Catcliffe the tower of the so-called Glass Cone remains, the oldest kiln (1740) in Europe, attracted by coal and the distribution facilities of the Don Navigation. Only three such cones survive. Its special products, manufactured up to 1901, were bottles and window glass. During the First World War it accommodated prisoners of war.

Rockley Furnace, near Worsbrough, built as early as 1652, was a charcoal blast furnace smelting hundreds of tons of iron ore each year.

From 1658 Wortley Top Forge used water power from the River Don, but the first record

The Catcliffe Cone.

was in 1621. From manufacturing iron for nails its range gradually expanded to railway components like axles. The Forge survived until 1929, becoming a museum from 1955, with original buildings, dams, waterwheels, hammers, cranes and steam engines on view.

INEXPERIENCED ARCHITECTS

There have been some odd instances of lay persons appointed as serious architects. James Paine (1717-1789) was still a teenager (nineteen) when commissioned by Sir Rowland Winn, 4th baronet, to modify and implement James Moyser's designs for Nostell Priory, on the site of a monastery dissolved by Henry VIII. He spent eight years on the main block of what was to become a Palladian masterpiece, with additional wings by Robert Adam. Furnishings include many pieces by a mature Thomas Chippendale, Otley's most celebrated son. Paine also designed Doncaster's Mansion House, 1748, as a residence for the mayor. Only two others exist – York and London.

Cuthbert Brodrick (1821-1905) won renown for three Leeds buildings. He was almost unknown when he won a £200 competition in 1852 to build a town hall. On the occasion of its opening by Queen Victoria on 7 September 1858 an estimated thirty-two thousand Sunday School children joined in the celebrations on Woodhouse Moor.

Three years later for another competition he designed the Corn Exchange (inspired by le Halle au Ble in Paris) and Mechanics Institute. More triumphs were to come, including the Grand Hotel, Scarborough in 1867; yet, having achieved national recognition, he decided to retire early to Paris. He died in Jersey.

INNOVATORS AND INVENTORS

Samuel Marsden was born at Farsley (1764) but emigrated as a chaplain to Parramatta, New South Wales in 1793. He involved himself heavily in sheep farming, as well as missionary work. And, significantly for West Yorkshire, he introduced Australian wool – from a Suffolk breed, interestingly – back to England in 1807. It was made into cloth by Messrs W. and J. Thompson of Park Mills, Rawdon. King George III had a suit made from it, and in return gave Marsden five Spanish Merino sheep to take Down Under.

Some inventions have been of pivotal significance for industrial development. Benjamin Huntsman was a Doncaster clockmaker who, around 1740, invented cast steel via a crucible process to which alloy elements could be added. By 1851 Sheffield was producing 86 per cent of English cast steel.

Then there were improvements which gradually became conventional necessities. In the early nineteenth century there were many established match manufactories. Richard Seanor perhaps tempted fortune when, in 1840, he started production in a former stable at Rothwell: predictably, there was a fire. After gaining experience in London he returned to production back home in Rothwell, this time in brick premises. In the pursuit of the perfect safety match there were more conflagrations. Production continued until the firm sold out to Bryant and May in 1895.

Conisbrough Castle keep.

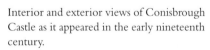

Interior and exterior views of Conisbrough
Castle as it appeared in the early nineteenth
century.

Not all inventions by West Yorkshiremen were concerned with industry. One that springs to mind was the Little Nipper Mouse trap with its deadly flip-back set on a small wooden base. It was the creation of James Henry Atkinson (1849-1942), a Leeds ironmonger who patented it in 1897. He sold the patent in 1913 for a thousand pounds to Procter Bros, a Welsh company who still manufacture it today.

Then there were sweetmeats. Liquorice, a tradition, an industry, a culture, a way of life is dealt with elsewhere. But there was that brand of toffee invented in Halifax by John and Violet Mackintosh, who opened their first sweetshop in King Cross Lane in 1890. They wanted it not too hard, like much English confectionery, nor too soft, like many American products. An old family recipe did the job, and early publicity was guaranteed by offering free samples. Prosperity followed, a factory was opened – and chocolate was added. During the Second World War William Joyce, or Lord Haw-Haw, the German propagandist alluded to Halifax as 'a certain toffee town'.

IVANHOE

Sir Walter Scott used Conisbrough Castle (calling it Coningsburgh) as a backdrop to his novel, written at nearby Sprotbrough in 1820, thereby putting it on the tourist route. He was first charmed by its romantic potential while travelling to London in a mail coach in 1811. This imagined Saxon castle was the home of the Lord Athelstane, who was revived from a deathly trance… and much more – the labyrinthine plot defies easy summary. The tale popularised the term 'War of the Roses'.

In a Leeds shopping arcade, Thornton's – the oldest (1877) – is a splendid clock with rotating animated characters from the book: the hours are struck by Richard the Lionheart and Friar Tuck, and the quarters by Robin Hood and Gurth the Swineherd.

JAW-DROPPING PANTO

In January 1924 Mrs Charles laughed so enthusiastically at the pantomime at Prince's Theatre, Shipley, that she dislocated her jaw! Fortunately her face was saved by doctors at St Luke's hospital.

JILTED

In 1807 William Sharp was jilted at the altar by his fiancée, Mary Smith, barmaid at the Devonshire Hotel, Keighley. Although she had already borne a son by him, their fathers opposed the match when a dowry couldn't be agreed. Devastated, thirty-year old William went home to Whorls Farm, at Laycock, and took to his bed for his remaining forty-nine years. … Only 9ft square and stone-flagged, the bedroom apparently offered little cheer or consolation. Still, William ate well, and had a nurse in attendance (who ensured he enjoyed an occasional change of bed linen). He died at the age of seventy-nine weighing seventeen stone.

JOBS

Things are not always what they seem. When a man called Horsfall died at Almondbury in 1639 the parish register described him as a 'pricker', .i.e. he pricked suspected witches with a needle: no bleeding meant further investigation.

For more recent job descriptions, how about these examples from the woollen industry:

Burlers were women who moved odd unwanted specks, vegetable bits, knots, tufts etc from woollen cloth.

Doffers took full bobbins from spinning frames and replaced them with empty bobbins.

Greasy perchers examined greasy cloth and prepared it for washing.

Slubbers removed knots after the carding of wool.

In long-established communities where most folk in the street knew one another, youngsters commonly did neighbourly errands for a few pence. Nowadays these transactions are rare. On leaving school some boys started off as errand lads, earning a living by delivering parcels etc for stationers, tailors, corner shops, or by doing odd jobs.

JOSEPH JAGGER (1830-92)

A spindle engineer at Shelf, near Bradford, Jagger treated himself, in 1875, to a holiday in Monte Carlo, where he visited the Beaux-Arts Casino. He became interested enough to hire six men to record successful numbers. Five roulette wheels showed random results, but a sixth seemed unduly to favour the numbers 7 8 9 17 18 19 22 28 29, probably owing to imperfectly balanced mechanisms, Joseph thought. He placed bets, and in four days won two million francs. When the management shifted the wheels round, Joseph started losing, before rediscovering his winning wheel. This time the inner workings were rejigged… and starting to lose again, he sensibly pulled out, to play no more. He continued to live at Shelf, gave up his job and invested in property.

Ironically, the hit song of 1892 – *The Man who Broke the Bank at Monte Carlo* – was aimed not at him, but at a more recent winning gambler.

JUDE FIREBACKED

Some divines are remembered for comparatively trivial acts rather than a lifetime of dedication and achievement. William Walsham How (1823-97), first Bishop of Wakefield from 1888, was a good bishop, a high churchman, keen on education and outdoor pursuits and the welfare of waifs and strays. (He was also a successful hymn writer, composing *For All The Saints*.) Yet he is apt to be remembered for writing to the *Yorkshire Post* in June 1896 supporting a recent article critical of the novelist Thomas Hardy: *Jude the Obscure* was, he protested, 'insolent and indecent' – and he had thrown it on the fire.

KETTY FAIR

It was customary on the last day of the ancient Wibsey horse fair in late November to dispose of old nags. Fair enough – so-be-it, some might say. But there were a few odd additional goings-on. Some older cows attracted the attention of women with jugs and sharp elbows seeking free milk. For the White Swan Inn dinner, goose keepers brewed their own beer, any leftover grains being fed to the 'Gooise Club'. Buyers needed to beware; many a shrewd purchaser found his nag, cow or goose changed colour during a shower.

'Ketty' probably derives from the Scandinavian *ket*, meaning carrion, offal, hence ketty – nasty, rancid.

KILLED BY THE CORONER

'John Jackson, a taylor of Leeds, was wounded at Skipton, and there dyed and was buried, after the coroner had satt on him.' (Skipton parish register, 19 December 1618.)

KIRKSTALL ABBEY

The abbey was founded by Henry de Lacy in the latter part of the twelfth century as a thanksgiving for his restored health. Lay brothers may have been the first organised miners in the area, digging coal for the forge. During the fourteenth century there was some intimidation of the locals involving the abbot, John de Thornberg. Evictions brought retaliatory arson, even deaths.

Whilst a promising trade in wool developed with Flanders and Italy, careless forward selling brought debts, compounded by a disease of flocks in the late thirteenth century.

Legend claims there were tunnels below this noble Cistercian foundation, linked to drinking houses! King Henry VIII may or may not have credited such rumours when he dissolved the Abbey in 1539. Centuries of neglect followed; by the end of the eighteenth century the main road into Leeds ran through the nave.

Col. J. T. North gave the estate to Leeds Corporation in 1889 so that the residents on Kirkstall Road could enjoy the parkland adjacent to the River Aire.

Inventive drainage channels percolated downwards from a higher placed mill pond, everything finishing in the river. The Reredorter, once a laybrothers' toilet, has been used as a smithy, a barn and, from late Victorian times until 1990, as a café. Nowadays it serves as a well-appointed visitors' centre.

KNOCKER-UP

Often a retired man from mill or mine, the knocker-up used a pole, wire fan, a brush or even an umbrella to knock at bedroom windows in order to rouse early workers. (Who woke the knocker-up?) The racket continued until someone drowsily declared he was up. It could be as early as 4.00 a.m. If a miner missed his cage he was sent home and lost his pay. Arthur Dodd served as knocker-up at Denaby Main for many years.

Kirkstall Abbey.

Eventually colliery buzzers came to announce the start and finish of a shift; and up to the outbreak of war in 1939 they also celebrated the New Year.

There were other means of awaking the workers. While at Normanton, 'Knocker' Eardley covered a considerable area and the 'Hope Street buzzer' was a donkey, somehow finely tuned to 4.30 a.m., which brayed the neighbourhood into wakefulness. At Ossett in mid-eighteenth century a horn was blown at 5 a.m. to 'get weaving', and at 8 p.m. to confirm the rest of the day was theirs. At Haworth until about 1914 a mill bell was tolled.

Occasionally we hear of a church bell proclaiming the end of a farming shift. This happened at Braithwell until the 1930s when a noon peal told farm workers to get ready for sandwiches/lunch/looance/dinner/snap/bait according to location and custom.

KNUR AND SPELL

The name may originate from the Norse *nurspel*, or *knur laijin* and could be of Viking origin. Traditionally it was played at Easter time and is still found at a few pubs around Halifax and Hebden Bridge and further north up to Skipton.

The skill in hitting the ball is not to be underestimated. When the knur (wooden ball) is sprung into the air from a brass cup (spell), the striker hits it as far as he can with a club weighted at the lower end. In mining areas the game was known as 'Poor Man's Golf', once drawing large crowds. At a Wibsey meeting, in May 1859, 10,000 supporters turned up.

Knur and spell (courtesy Heptonstall Museum). The bat (or pummel) is leaning on the left; angled upwards is the spell, or spring trap, for holding the knur ball.

Duties, like church going, were neglected. At the Wakefield Petty Sessions of February 1842 Richard Bramhall, John Ramsden and George Whittaker were each fined 1s for playing on a Sunday.

There were imitation games for children, like 'peggy', or 'nipsy', where a small stick, pointed at one end, was made to fly upwards and hit whilst airborne. The furthest won, although locally there were some complicated rituals other than strides.

LATER LUDDITES

Worker vendettas against the new machines continued into the twenties and thirties. For example, in 1826 power looms were damaged in Gargrave cotton mills; in 1834 handloom workers ambushed a loom on a journey between Keighley and Bradford. Eight years later, new power-driven machinery at Dewhurst and Sidgwick's mills, Skipton was sabotaged; the attack escalated into street looting, with soldiers called in to restore order.

LAUREATES THREE

West Yorkshire has produced three Poet Laureates:

1) Laurence Eusden (1688-1730), son of the rector of Spofforth. In 1718 he was appointed Laureate by Thomas Pelham-Holles, Duke of Newcastle, who had been poetically flattered on the occasion of his marriage. But there were acerbic critics, like Alexander Pope:

Eusden, a laurel'd Bard, by fortune rais'd
By very few was read, by fewer praised.

2) Born in Headingly, Alfred Austin (1835-1913) succeeded Tennyson as Laureate in 1896, and suffered by comparison. Caricaturists were not wanting – such as Frank Baum, who dubbed him 'Sir Austed Alfrin' in a novel, *John Dough and the Cherub*.

3) Ted Hughes, born at Mytholmroyd, was elevated as Laureate in 1984. Recent opinion quibbles less on his poetic merits than on controversies occasioned by the ladies in his life. Lumb Bank, Heptonstall, where Ted and his wife Carol lived during the 1970s, has become the Ted Hughes Arvon Centre for writers.

'PIE' LEACH (1815-1893)

James Leach traded in pies and groceries. He was given to nostalgia, notably at his third wedding at the age of seventy-six to a thirty-five year old lady, Margaret Bowes. Unfortunately, his nuptial oration at the Keighley Temperance Hall was devoted to the merits of his previous spouses!

In other ways he was a forward planner. During 1887, six years before his death, Pie prepared his own coffin, and duly erected his tombstone in the Skipton Road Cemetery.

LECTURE SUNDAY

Up to mid-Victorian times some Heckmondwike chapels held a June Lecture Sunday, with special sermons and invitations extended to outlying congregations to join in. For this gala event, houses were spring cleaned for family gatherings, with gingerbread samplings and even a 'lecture pud' prepared in celebration.

LEEDS FAIR SAMARITANS

'The Soup Establishment is in active operation only in times of peculiar distress… There are in Leeds also two or three Clothing Societies, by which benevolent females of the more opulent and middle classes supply their poor neighbours with garments, which these fair Samaritans make with their own hands.' (Baines's *Yorkshire*, Vol. I, 1822.)

LEEDS IMPROVEMENT COMMISSION

1833 Report – 'From the privies in the Boot and Shoe Yard (Kirkgate) which did not appear to have been thoroughly cleansed for the last thirty years, 70 cart loads of manure were removed by order of the Commissioners.'

This Yard suffered from the familiar deprivation of overcrowding, poor light and ventilation, lack of sanitation… and a drain emanating from the adjacent pig market. Complaints gathered momentum…

Leodis is an old name for Leeds.

LEEDS IMPROVEMENT ACT, 1842

This measure aimed at (among other things) prohibiting refuse from being pitched from windows into the street, the keeping of pigs in houses, and the letting of cellars with no windows or fireplaces. Not to be outdone, Bradford Corporation shortly adopted a bye-law with similar provisions. Yet despite the ravages of cholera, councillors dismissed the limewashing of poor dwellings as too expensive.

Domestic pig-keeping was a ubiquitous problem. At Skipton, Piggy Sam was a character strenuously avoided, as he kept a herd of pigs in his residence on Mill Bridge.

LEEDS LOINERS

Who are they? Natives of Leeds, of course, and proud of it! Why 'loiners', though? Some aver that loins were lanes, like some off Briggate. Others have suggested a link with loins of cotton cloth. Then again, the Venerable Bede of Jarrow, as far back as the eighth century, had called the district 'Loidis'. In medieval times this became 'Leedis.' Sometimes there is no clear answer to these questions. You might as well ask what that City Square landmark, the equestrian statue of Edward the Black Prince, has to do with the city's history. The blunt answer is nowt! (And if you're one of these off-comed-uns, unfortunate enough not to be born a loiner, what's it matter to you, anyroad?)

LEGENDS

In order to preserve the bones of St Cuthbert of Lindisfarne against Viking invaders, about the year AD 875 monks visited Fishlake, the most southerly resting place of their quest (hence the unusual dedication of the parish church). Eventually, in AD 995 the saint was interred at Durham.

The Bawtry saddler, *en route* to his York execution, spurned a last drink at the 'Gallows House' hostelry. Had he requested his cart to stop, he might have benefited from a last-minute reprieve.

According to a later seventeenth-century poetic satire, The Dragon of Wantley lived in the crags of Wharncliffe, creating terror and eating children and cattle, until the knight More killed it. The poem was based on real-life grievances: Wantley was Wharncliffe; the dragon was Sir Francis Wortley, an extortionate landlord who destroyed farms, appropriated land and imposed unfair tithes. Lawyer More of More Hall won a legal challenge, bringing relief to the parish.

Rombald, fleeing from an enemy, trampled on a rock near Ilkley, splitting it into two sections, subsequently called the Cow and Calf. The enemy turned out to be... his wife!

While drinking at a well a ferocious wild boar was shot by bow and arrow in Cliffe Wood near medieval Bradford. To claim the reward for ridding the area of the beast, the huntsman, John Northrop Manningham, cut out its tongue and headed for the manor house. A second man, seeing the carcass, cut its head off, and he too went to stake his claim, but his tale wasn't accepted. Manningham, arriving later with the tongue, was found worthy, and received land, now modern Horton – hence Bradford's coat-of-arms includes a boar's head without the tongue, seated on top of a well. He and his heirs were to blow three blasts on a hunting horn every St Martin's Day (11 November).

A famous mulberry bush grew within the precincts of Wakefield prison. Inmates trooping around it for recreation is one explanation of the well-known children's rhyme. Another suggestion is that female prisoners once made it a focus of walks with their young children.

A wild cat and Sir Percival Cresacre fought to their mutual deaths in the porch of St Peter's church, Barnburgh, in around 1477, after a running battle – hence the Cat and Man effigy in the Cresacre Chapel.

LEGGIN' IT

The Standedge Tunnel was gouged through Pennine millstone grit from Marsden to Diggle in order to take the Huddersfield Narrow Canal to Ashton-under-Lyne. Begun by Benjamin Outram in 1794, the project was soon taken over by Thomas Telford. It is the UK's longest canal tunnel (3 miles 135 yards), the deepest cut (645ft underground at the deepest point), and the highest above sea-level (640ft).

Hundreds of navvies worked at both ends blasting and digging. There were fears that they might not meet: the tunnel, opened in 1811, has a few bends! To reduce costs there was no tow path, so boatmen lay on their backs in the darkness, digging their clogs and boots into the roof and tunnel sides so as to propel the barge forward. The journey could take four hours! Unemployed men often stood near the entrance, ready for hire as leggers.

Unharnessed horse teams had to be led over the hill to the opposite tunnel exit by company employees or children. In a long career (1811-52) as boat supervisor, or 'Standedge Admiral,' Thomas Bourne walked approximately 217,500 miles, crossing Standedge four times a day.

LEISURE PURSUITS

Eighteenth-century feast days were often riotous. Clog fighters standing on opposite sides of a horizontal bar held onto it, kicking each other until one yielded. Skelmanthorpe villagers were keen on dog fights, bull and bear baiting, bare-knuckle fights. Cock-fighting was widespread... and occasionally one even reads of rat pits!

Now and again animals wreaked vengeance. Septimus Lister of Ecclesfield recorded in his diary that on 11 December 1790 a bear escaped from his ward, William Cooper, at High Green, entered a house and attacked a mother there, one Mary Rogers: she died of her wounds the following Monday. The animal was shot.

Over a century ago colliers enjoyed arrow-throwing competitions. Eating competitions were popular, as at Morley Feast in 1842 when many plates of hot 'lumpy dicks,' or hasty puddings, ensured the prize was won by the 'King of Eaters' (name unrecorded but described as a sort of cannibal) of Turvin Vale.

If nothing special was afoot men might resort to racing greyhounds, whippets, ferrets and pigeons. But there were also a few aesthetic musical attractions (apart from brass bands) such as the Brighouse Lark Singing Association, which held contests with live birds in the 1890s. Choosing winners must have been an invidious task for judges.

For the more sedate tastes there were, for instance, Band of Hope activities, walking, cricket, Mutual Improvement societies, Mechanics Institutes and choirs.

LINDEN LEA

The music to William Barnes' famous words was written by Ralph Vaughan Williams in 1902 during a visit to his friend, the Revd R.A. Gatty, an antiquarian of Hooton Roberts.

LISTER'S PRIDE

Lister's Mill (Manningham Mills) was the creation of Samuel Cunliffe Lister (1815-1906). With floor space of 27 acres it became the biggest silk mill in the world. It has a 255ft tall chimney, which Lister climbed on the first working day in 1873 to open a bottle of champagne. Modelled on the bell tower of San Marco, Venice, it still dominates the city's northern skyline.

A four months' strike from December 1890 gave impetus to the formation of the Bradford Labour Union; and shortly to the Independent Labour Party in 1893. Although the workers were starved back to work, they had learnt lessons in organisation.

In 1904 Lister was created Lord Masham. His prosperity continued. For the coronation of King George V (1910) he was given an order for 1,000 yards of velvet. With changing conditions, especially foreign competition and the use of man-made fibres, his successors were forced out of business by the 1990s. The mill has recently been converted into flats.

LITTLE GERMANY

During the 1820s and 1830s this handsome warehouse area was built on a slope behind Bradford Cathedral by enterprising German merchants importing wool and exporting cloth. Although for cost-cutting reasons they wanted to use their own premises, rather than the Wool Exchange, many were of philanthropic bent. Julius Delius, a wool broker from Germany, and father of the composer (and thirteen other children) had such a warehouse, and was a sponsor for the Bradford Children's Hospital. Charles Semon, ex-Danzig, helped hospitals and became the first foreign (and Jewish) Mayor of Bradford in 1910.

Bradford had earlier immigrants from Germany, as indicated in such quarters as Bonn Road, Heidelberg Road and Mannheim Road. Leeds, twinned with Dortmund, has a Dortmund Square in which stands the Beermaker, or Barrel Man statue, dedicated in 1980, and is a symbol of Dortmund's main industry – brewing. In return the German city has developed a Leeds Platz (Square).

Recent re-development of Little Germany has been for offices and residential use.

LITTLE MESTERS

Essentially the term has been used of small units of Sheffield cutlers. Well into the nineteenth century small metal workshops with only a few workers continued to exist alongside big mills and factories, like Thomas Firth & Sons, established in 1842. The area around Silsden, just north of Keighley, specialised in nail making, with many small masters with their own smithies, and a few workmen. There was, too, part-time labour from local farms. Smithies often attracted locals who dropped in for a chat, or to have some literate friend read bits from the newspapers. 'Little Mesters' workshops can be seen at the Kelham Island Industrial Museum, Sheffield.

Moreover, especially in the Aire and Calder valleys, there were 'little makers', i.e. wool weavers, small clothier craftsmen working in their stone cottages on their own looms and materials, and carrying their finished products to Halifax or Leeds. They employed spinners, often members of the family. The lifestyle fostered independence – and plain speaking. They gradually disappeared with the growing ascendancy of factories and merchant capitalists.

LIQUORICE

This leguminous shrub may have been brought to Pontefract from the Middle East following the Crusades. It was used for medicinal purposes, and recommended for anti-inflammatory and stomach-calming properties. Gargling with a liquorice solution was said to help sore throats. By the seventeenth century there were liquorice garths (fields) flourishing in the town's sandy soil. In 1760 a chemist, George Dunhill, made Pomfret cakes, adding sugar to liquorice (and the crest of a gateway and an owl). By the 1880s increasing demand drew imports from Spain, hence the term 'Spanish.' Palm Sunday was appropriated as Liquorice Day.

For several reasons (changes in taste, competition from chocolate, dearer imports from China and Turkey) there was a post-war decline, though some market gardens survived into the 1960s. John Betjeman's poem *The Licorice Fields at Pontefract* lent a romantic glow to the industry. A modern festival is held in February.

LODGERS

The accelerating migration of the early nineteenth century from countryside to the industrial towns brought much squalor, deprivation and multi-tenancies. About 1850, an example was quoted in Huddersfield of twenty lodgers sharing different shifts and four beds; in Halifax, nineteen lodgers had no beds. Robert Baker, a factory inspector, reported of Bradford – 'in many cellars not four yards square... fifteen, sixteen and twenty people preparing to pass the night, persons of both sexes, strangers to each other in the same room, in the same bed, on the same floor...'

In the 1840s in Keighley there was an instance of one privy shared by twenty-nine houses. The Medical Officer of Health for Normanton in his report for 1884 referred to a small terraced house on Scarborough Row where the family numbers had been swollen by fourteen lodgers. Some music-hall jokes were, indeed, founded on fact!

LODDY

Laudanum (opium dissolved in alcohol) was used to lull infants to sleep, so that mothers could get to work. It was much abused, and not only in respect of the very young. It contributed to the downfall of Branwell Brontë, for example, who bribed folk to buy supplies for him from local chemists – who knew him and might refuse.

LONGEVITY

Despite life's hardships a few folk lived into considerable old age; an inscription in the chancel of St Peter's church at Thorner mentions John Philips, 1625-1742.

Isabel and James Robinson, buried in St Martin's churchyard, Firbeck, had combined ages of 220 years. Isabel of Stone died in 1694 aged 111; when her son James passed on in 1730 his years were 109.

LOO LARGESSE

In June 1896 the Rothwell School Board commissioned a number of four-seater trough closets for its schools, thus blurring the distinction between private and public communing.

LUDDENDEN MAYOR-MAKING

It started as recently as 1996 with a September election near the Lord Nelson Inn. The robed mayor makes a mock attack on the 'wicked' Calderdale Council, pledging not to include Halifax in his/her postal address. This little bit of street theatre deliberately looks back to the 1860s when the village refused to be taken over by the local government of Halifax. Funds are raised through a barbecue, stalls, duck race, auction, etc.

MACE MEN

Arthur Monjoy was a silversmith of Briggate, Leeds. He made the town's silver mace, but was hanged at York in 1696 for coining.

Although Joseph Ratcliffe had been involved in the infamous Luddite attack on Cartright's Mill in 1812, he turned informer and good citizen, holding office as Beadle and Mace-bearer in Halifax.

MAPPLEWELL AND STAINCROSS SING

Every year since 1887 on the third Sunday in July a large sing-along (especially hymns and excerpts from Handel's *Messiah*) has taken place at Staincross near Barnsley to raise money for hospitals. Traditionally the occasion has been part of 'Feast Week and Sing'.

Noteworthy, too, is the Mollicarr Woods Sing on Whitsunday which, hail, rain or shine, begins briskly at 7.30 a.m! These alfresco proceedings started with the Zion Chapel, Almondbury, in 1900; the chapel wanted to practise without disturbing their neighbours. Three stops are made in the bluebell woods to sing hymns and a charity collection ends the proceedings.

MARITAL MULLARKEY

Adam Eyre had served under General Fairfax in the Parliamentary Army during the Civil War. Later, from Hazlehead, Sheffield, his diary, 1646-8, shows insights into his relations with his wife, Susan. His fondness for the alehouse and male companionship having brought tensions and money worries, he resolved to spend more time at home.

May 26 1647: 'I blooded my wife in her sore foot, which bled very well…'

8 June: 'This morn my wife began, after her old manner, to brawl and revile me for wishing her only to wear such apparel as was decent and comely and accused me of treading on her sore foot… at dinner I told her I purposed never to come to bed with her till she took more notice of what I formerly had said to her.'

11 August: Following a visit to Barnsley, despite making various purchases including 10d worth of tobacco for his lady and giving her 10 shillings, 'at night she kept the gates shut and said she would be master of the house for that night.'

Then, as now, wars, whether military or marital, tend to be uncivil!

MARKET PLACE SCULPTURE

Near the market place steps in Batley is a captivating sculpture, in sandstone and bronze, depicting aspects of the town's life – a Rugby boot, books including a *History of Batley*, and bales and rolls of cloth. The creation, by local sculptors Malcolm Haigh and Janet Lubinska, was mounted in 1999.

MARRYING INTO MONEY?

Son of an improvident barrister who abandoned the law to become a bankrupt farmer, Anthony Trollope, after a miserable childhood, sought the security of a job with the Post Office. While working as a PO surveyor in Ireland he met Rose Heseltine, on holiday with her family. He no doubt brightened on finding out that her father was Edward John Heseltine, manager of the Sheffield and Rotherham Joint Stock Banking Co. The wedding took place on 11 June 1844 in All Saints church, Rotherham.

Alas, the young husband soon began to have doubts. Not only did the family live modestly above the shop, but Edward J's financial records revealed irregularities, then deficits… and he fled to France. Fortunately, Anthony proved himself a literary workaholic, and over the years established a permanent name with the Barchester novels, *The Way We Live Now*, etc. And he probably made a bob or two with the invention of the Post Office pillar box.

MARSDEN CUCKOO DAY

This annual celebration during the third week in April recalls the legend of the villagers who tried to wall in their well-loved bird, hoping for perpetual warm springs and summers. When the bird flew off, recriminations set in – 'Wall were nobbut just one course too low!' A procession with a giant cuckoo and children with cuckoo hats tours the village, and there is clog dancing and a duck race.

Sculpture, Batley market place.   Maypole, Barwick in Elmet.

Skipton once had a tradition of ' huntin' ti gowk' (cuckoo), or sending some naïve person on a hoax errand.

MAYPOLES

Every year Gawthorpe's ribbon plaiting ceremony, with a May Queen, band and procession, attracts crowds on the first Saturday in May. Barwick in Elmet is thought to have had a maypole for centuries. Their Whit Monday merrymaking takes place every third year, after the pole has been repainted white with red and blue stripes, and garlanded with flowers. Topped with a polished metal fox, it rises to a height of 86ft.

Traditionally some poles have been stolen by neighbouring villages. When the Gawthorpe pole was taken by Chickenly in 1850, repercussions were serious, with a brawl causing one death and serious injuries. Barwick's has had to be recovered from Aberford in times past, but nowadays carries an electronic burglar alarm.

Before the term 'headbanger' was in common parlance, the expression somehow arose 'knocked at Barwick,' referring to a weak, or weakened, intellect incurred, perhaps, during a shifting of the pole, lawfully or otherwise.

MECHANICS INSTITUTES

Cynics might claim that these establishments served to divert the workers from pubs and gambling, but evening classes, talks, meetings, and reading rooms gained early prominence in West Yorkshire. Leeds was to the fore with a hall in 1824, and others soon followed in Halifax, Huddersfield, Bradford, Dewsbury and Keighley. While the movement was slower in reaching smaller towns, by 1861 Marsden, near Huddersfield, was offering classes in grammar, composition, arithmetic, geography, science and singing.

MELTHAM SINGERS

Once upon a time the group would often seem to begin in the wrong key – with some parts of the audience actually willing them so to do – and would suffer all the embarrassment of having to start again. According to some critics their conductor, Matthew, could not always be exonerated!

MILLERS

Chaucer's miller had some unattractive traits. His successors, too, drove hard bargains with gullible folk. With more cynical trades the profession invited obloquy and derision: carters and boatmen transporting a miller's sack often did so grudgingly. Not only was the last miller at Mill Hill, Normanton, one Charles Haugh, noted for his bad temper; reputedly he hadn't washed for ten years. For some parishioners the blowing down of his mill in a gale in 1837 seemed to be Providential correction.

MILL TALK

The volume of decibels became proverbial: Rattle Row, Holmfirth derived directly from the noise of handlooms. Youngsters coming to work in the mills soon learned to depend on lip reading, gestures – and, situations permitting, the occasional familiar rude exchange, possibly at the expense of immediate supervisors.

Initiation ceremonies created much humour for established workers. In some textile mills the nipper's face was greased with an oily cloth. Then there were hoax errands, on the lines of 'Get thissen ti Jonty's ower yonder an' bring back a pennorth o' pigeon milk, a spirit level bubble, some strop oil an' a round square. Oh aye – an' a bucket o' steam. Has gorrit?'

This is said in particular of Bingley folk: 'If they can induce a greenhorn to fetch a pennorth o' strop oil from the grocer's, or the second edition of Cock Robin from the bookseller's, their delight is unbounded.' (James Burnley, *West Riding Sketches*, 1875)

The mills provided one permanent cultural outlet – clog dancing, which probably began with the workers tapping their feet to the rhythm of the machines, improvised entertainment growing out of it. Nowadays there is a summer festival at Skipton.

MINING FAMILIES

What a special breed, those generations of lads who followed their fathers down t' pit. The job bred camaraderie. They understood one another, depended on one another for safety – the dangers were legion, including insecure props, gas, and explosions (many caused through colliers' candles igniting fire-damp gas, as happened at the Jane Pit, Rothwell in 1882). Much worse was the epic tragedy at the Old Oaks Colliery, Barnsley on 13 October 1866, when 361 men and boys were killed in explosions. Twenty-seven of the rescuers also died.

Roof falls were commonplace, often due to shot-firing repercussions or props collapsing. Every miner had blue scars on his body, frequently on his face, arms, shoulders and legs.

Working conditions were atrocious, especially before the era of mechanisation, coal-cutters and conveyors. When the cage reached the usually whitewashed pit bottom, there was generally a walk to the coal face – sometimes for a mile or two as further seams were opened. Some seams were less than two feet thick – and there in the most cramped conditions men laboured, somehow, with pick and shovel. For the duration of the shift they inhaled dust. They often worked in ankle-deep water. The story may not be altogether apocryphal of the miner – could it have been at Gomersal Colliery? – who floated a plastic duck on a big puddle, tossing bits of bread to it, to draw the attention of a visiting mines inspector. An' hey-up, what were that? Toilets, did tha say?

True, the workers received concessionary coal (which was dumped outside their house, on the footpath (coursey) or in the road). Bigger lads (or even a hefty wife) might help to carry large lumps and place them at the sides of the coalhouse. After his shift the man had to wheel in the rest of the load, before the luxury of his fireside tub bath. It was a wife's daily chore to scrub shoulders and parts of the back which the husband couldn't reach. What a blessing pit-head baths were, mostly after the mines were nationalised.

Behind the pit-head winding gear huge slag heaps piled up. During hard times, like strikes, some folk ventured with buckets to pick out any usable bits. One prospector at Wath-on-Dearne during the 1926 strike was ten-year old Dennis Parkin, who, after working as a pit lad, was eventually commissioned into the West Yorkshire Regiment and won the DSO fighting the Japanese in Burma.

With tied houses the property of coal owners, there was always the fear of eviction if men withdrew their labour. It happened during a strike at Denaby Main in 1903; and two years later at Kinsley, near Hemsworth. At Methley National School it was

Grieving miner's widow, Conisbrough – a tribute to the men and boys who died at Denaby and Cadeby Main Collieries, and to the women who suffered their loss.

recorded: 'Owing to the strike Mr Briggs, the coal proprietor, has turned parents and children out of his houses and great destitution has been caused in the village in consequence'. In these hard times Salvation Army soup kitchens kept many a family going.

There were some consolations in these tight-knit communities: stoicism, humour, galas, brass bands, choirs, sport, pigeons, dogs… though shift work generally militated against social life. No wonder many miners liked their pint.

Since 1995 the old Caphouse Colliery, near Wakefield, has served as a museum, with a team of ex-miners acting as attendants. Visitors are invited into the pit cage, which drops 450ft, to begin to see what conditions were like. Half-wheels from former head-gear have been mounted as memorials in a number of villages near Wakefield (e.g. at Sharlston Colliery, 1865-1993).

MISCHIEF NAYT

It became institutionalised for 4 November. There was little vandalism or destruction: the odd gate might be lifted, a few door knobs smeared with grease or treacle, doors knocked on by young villains who then ran away – or rope ends tied on two adjacent doors in the terrace, knocks on both and a retreat to watch the outcome. But the local community code generally ensured that old folk, widows and the lame suffered no harassment.

MODERN SCULPTORS

Born at Castleford, the seventh child of a mining engineer, Henry Moore (1898-1986) attended the Leeds School of Art, where he was the first student of sculpture. Here he met Barbara Hepworth and they became lifetime friends. Henry has become especially noted for making sculpture 'the art of open air', with Earth Mother themes, and abstract figures cast in bronze or carved in marble. Many figures are reclining, like that outside Castleford Civic Centre; and the voluptuous lady luring in passers-by at

Reclining lady
by Henry Moore,
Castleford.

the entrance to Leeds Art Gallery. His election to Companion of Honour and Order of Merit were recognitions of his achievements during his lifetime. The Henry Moore Institute and Gallery is situated in Leeds.

Barbara Hepworth (1903-1975) was born at Wakefield. She, too, helped to establish the Modernist approach with an astonishing series of curving and sensual abstracts. She became Dame Barbara in 1965.

Remarkable, too, are several of their friends and contemporaries who attended Castleford Grammar School. They include the novelist J.L. Carr; Albert Wainwright, painter and illustrator, creator of theatre stage sets and costumes; and Arthur Dalby, who became one of His Majesty's Inspectors for Art in schools. All acknowledge an inspirational debt to their teacher, Alice Gostick.

MONDAY WASH

Monday was – is – the traditional wash day. Our grandmothers will recall the problems of heating up water, in the set pot or a brick boiler, with a fire needing to be kept well-stoked to heat the water. In those primitive days before soap powders, grated soap and soda crystals were added, and everything agitated and stirred round with a four-legged dolly (or peggy stick), and a posser, or plunger, for pounding. Really dirty clothes had to be treated separately on a rubbing board. After rinsing, with much wrist twisting, came the mangle with a big wheel to turn its rollers – a sustained effort with heavy wet clothes.

Hanging out presented more problems. Sometimes in areas with little garden space, as with Leeds back-to-backs, there were neighbourly agreements (and occasional disagreements) regarding washing lines slung across the street. At Saltaire, however, these were forbidden as unsightly by Sir Titus Salt. Still, in the communal wash-house he had placed six steam-driven washing machines and even a spin drier! Few folk elsewhere were so lucky.

On fine days garments were taken out in the voider (basket) and strewn on bushes. Occasionally churchyard tombstones might be used. This happened at Haworth until stopped in 1847 by the Revd Arthur Nicholls, husband of Charlotte Brontë.

In winter or on rainy days the washing had to be hung about the house to dry. The atmosphere was still steamy when the men came in from work. Many weren't best pleased.

Next day was ironing. With flat irons heated at the front of the fire there was always the fear of scorching the linen. Warm work indeed.

In some villages one or two women took in, additionally, soiled laundry from the Big House!

LADY MARY WORTLEY MONTAGU (1689-1762)

Famous for her wit, poetry and letters, Mary was brought up partly in Yorkshire, and married Edward Wortley Montagu in 1712. One of their homes was Wortley Hall, near Sheffield. She accompanied Edward to Constantinople on his appointment as ambassador. Having suffered smallpox, she had her four-year-old son inoculated in Turkey, somewhat controversially; and well before the pioneer work of Dr Edward

Jenner (1796) she introduced the idea back in England. In Wentworth Castle grounds stands an obelisk recording her intellectual achievements.

MOONRAKERS

In 1802, Slaithwaite (pronounced Slawit) smugglers hid barrels of rum and whisky amid canal reeds, away from the customs men. If caught at night hauling the booty out with rakes they would claim, with feigned stupidity, that they were 'raking the moon', hoping to capture its reflection. An annual February festival, with a procession of lanterns, re-enacts the tale, followed by a fireworks display.

MYSTERY PLAYS

The term comes from the French word *metier*, meaning trade. From the late fourteenth century until 1576 the Wakefield Cycle of plays was generally held in the Cathedral precincts at Corpus Christi in June.

Thirty-two plays or pageants were drawn from Bible stories, including Noah, Jonah, and the birth and resurrection of Christ. Originally each guild took a story congenial to its trade (e.g. woodworkers took Noah's Ark). A wagon sometimes made a convenient stage. Although the scripts were basically serious, some comic elements became an expected feature. In the *Second Shepherds' Play*, after a thief stole a lamb and tried to pass it off as a baby in a cradle, he was tossed in a blanket. Wagons have been used in recent revivals.

NAMES

Situated in a Pennine bowl once dotted with chimneys, Halifax was known as the Devil's Cauldron. Other odd-sounding places are Jump (between Hoyland and Wombwell), and Idle (near Bradford), mention of which inevitably leads to arch comments about the Idle Working Men's Club. Then we have the River Idle at Bawtry, a former inland port long idle! Meanwhile, Egypt, Moscow and World's End are hamlets near Thornton.

Skipton in Anglo-Saxon times was 'Sceptun' – sheep town. The wool link was to last for centuries. Swinton was 'swine farm', ancient Latin documents referring to Villa Porcorum (House of Pigs). Brockholes could only be the domain of badgers.

Fourteenth-century Doncaster had Friendless Street, possibly because of unpleasant trades like leather tanning. We can gather something of Pontefract's medieval past from its street names – Beast Fair, Shoe Market, Salter Row, Rope Gate. Otley has Walkergate, where finishers of woollen cloth literally 'walked' on the material. Less explicably, Bradford has 'All Alone'. In Heptonstall, Top o' th Town is a touch of dialect. There is much localised pronunciation too: 'Yetton' for Kirkheaton; 'Goker' (Golcar); Gawthrup (Gawthorpe); and Slawit for Slaithwaite.

Some names have been invented. Bruddersford was J.B. Priestley's name for Bradford in novels like *The Good Companions* and *Bright Day*. He also devised

'Cleckheckmondsedge', a generic mishmash for Cleckheaton/ Heckmondwike/ Liversedge. Of anonymous origin is the snide variation of 'Cleckuddersfax', denoting Cleckheaton, Huddersfield and Halifax.

Narrow alleyways, or short cuts, are ginnels and snickets. In the old back-to-backs of Leeds and Bradford, 'gooin' dahn ginnel' meant proceeding to the lavatory, which might well have been communal.

Butts Green near Luddenden and Kell Butts, Wainstalls remind us that younger men were once required by law to do regular archery practice.

The pub known as 'Dick Hudson's' is actually the Fleece Inn at High Eldwick. A family of Hudsons were landlords in Victorian times, the famous Dick reigning for thirty years from 1850. Traditionally it has been a walkers' stop-off for ham and eggs.

Once it seemed that almost everyone had a nickname. Bill o'Hoylus End was the pen-name of William Wright (1836-97), soldier, woolcomber, strolling actor, playwright and dialect writer of Victorian times, famous for comical accounts of local folk and their doings; and Hoylus End is at Hermit Hole, near Keighley. 'Peg Leg' was a 1930s exhibitionist who hopped up a ladder, then dived into a large tank in Roundhay Park, Leeds. There were some groupings, too, like 'Crooked-legged uns' (i.e. mill workers whose limbs were damaged by their conditions of servitude).

Even a few collieries acquired unexpected names. At East Garforth the Isabella and Elizabeth pits were sunk in 1833, named after ladies of the mine owners, the Gascoignes.

And a curious coincidence: Bradford's Peace Museum (peace history, conflict resolution, etc.) is located in Piece Hall Yard, BD1 1PJ!

Oh, and Haworth is twinned with Machu Picchu, Peru.

NELSON OF PONTEFRACT

Covering most of the south wall of the court room in the old town hall (1785) is a gigantic plaster cast of the death of Nelson aboard HMS *Victory*. It was used for a panel at the foot of the Trafalgar Square column. Benjamin Oliveira MP, a friend of the sculptor, I.E. Carew, suggested to the mayor that it might look well in Pontefract. His Worship agreed, and in December 1855 the cast was laboriously transported in six sections by horse and cart. Christmas euphoria evaporated, however, when the bill arrived, covering costs of transportation and installation. Oliveira's name was deleted from the accompanying plaque. The size of the bill, reluctantly paid, was never disclosed.

NEWLAND'S MILL DISASTER

Sir Henry Ripley built a huge chimney for his mill at West Bowling, Bradford, 1862. He was determined it should be imposing – and at 255ft it was. But it needed many repairs – some claimed it leaned – and it didn't last. After a storm on 28 December 1882 4,000 tons of brickwork fell, killing fifty-four women and children. A plaque was erected in 2002.

NEW YEAR DIP

Since the 1960s this chilly event has taken place on the first Sunday in January at Lee Dam, Lumbutts near Todmorden. Men, women and children splash around in the hope of winning wooden cups and raising money for charity.

Folk around here must be a hardy breed. On 20 April 1890 a prize fight was held nearby lasting thirty-six bruising rounds.

NOCTURNAL FUNERALS

In many households on the eve of burial, the corpse was watched over in the front room (parlour), with candles lit at the head and foot of the coffin. Up to about 1800 in the Skipton area, women who had died in childbirth were sometimes buried at night. So were some suicides and paupers.

But torchlit processions to the graveside were quite customary for the gentry and yeomanry. For many years the coffins of the Kitchenman family of Allerton Hall, Chapeltown, Leeds were carried by torchlight for burial in St Peter's church. We read in the diary of Oliver Heywood, 1681: 'Lady Rodes of Houghton, a great upholder of meetings, buried at Darfield April 21st at 12 in the night aged 72'.

Above: Nelson of Pontefract, Town Hall.

Right: Number One, Yorkshire – that famous door, Bawtry.

'NUMBER ONE, YORKSHIRE'

On entering Bawtry from Notts off the Great North Road, the first house on the right, the southernmost in Yorkshire, carries the legend 'Number one, Yorkshire'. It was the custom for the sheriff to welcome royalty at Bawtry. In 1541 Sir Robert Bowes, with 200 gents and 4,000 yeomen, met Henry VIII, giving him a purse holding with 900 pounds in gold.

The town, on the River Idle, describes itself as a twelfth-century port. Its church is dedicated to St Nicholas, patron saint of seafarers. Early exports to the continent were of wool. By the 1540s John Leland described the town as 'very bare and pore'. But it revived with the export of millstones, and smelted lead from the Sheffield area, some of it transported via the Trent and Humber to Hull and shipped to Amsterdam. It later became a staging post on the Great North Road.

NUTTY CRACK NAYT

On Halloween (31 October) certain divination games were played by practical jokers and the superstitious. If two nuts burned well together in a fire's embers, all was well. If they cracked or flew apart a young couple faced trouble. Nuts, or apple pips, could be squeezed between finger and thumb to fly towards a likely future partner.

OAK APPLE DAY

The 29 May commemorated the escape of the future Charles II from the Battle of Worcester – he famously hid in an oak tree at Boscobel in 1651. To celebrate, folk sported oak leaves: children not doing so would suffer nettle stings, as many grandparents will recall. This day was also the king's birthday and the day he returned in triumph to London in 1660, after eleven years of 'Commonwealth tyranny'.

OASTLER'S LETTER

The famous letter on Yorkshire Child Slavery, written by Richard Oastler (1789-1861), land steward at Fixby Hall near Huddersfield, was printed in the *Leeds Mercury* on 16 October 1830.

'The very streets of our towns are every morning wet with the tears of innocent victims at the accursed shrine of avarice, who are compelled not by the cart whip of the negro slave driver, but by the dread of the equally appalling thong or strap of the overlooker, to hasten half-dressed, but not half-fed, to those magazines of British infantile slavery, the worsted mills of the town of Bradford.'

A campaign was mounted, with support crossing normal party allegiances. John Fielden, for example, was a benevolent Todmorden millowner. In general Oastler himself claimed high Tory, not radical, views, but he joined a protest march with 12,000 men on York Castle. While in the Fleet prison for debt, he continued to work for reduced working hours for factory children. Funds were raised to free him.

Finally, the Factory Act of 1833 prohibited the employment of children less than nine years of age; those between nine and thirteen would work a maximum of nine hours a day; and there was to be no night work for youngsters under eighteen. Government inspectors were to be appointed.

OLDEST

Originating in around AD 905, the Bingley Arms, Bardsey claims to be the oldest pub in England. Until 1780 it was the Priests Inn, supposedly because of former links with Kirkstall Abbey; it was a resting place for monks en route for St Mary's Abbey, York.

Lee Gap Fair, West Ardsley, once lasting for three weeks and three days, is England's oldest horsefair, going back to the twelfth century and granted by Royal Charter to Nostell Priory. A priest was often available to marry couples impatient for the customary banns. Stories abound of quarrels, fights, drunkenness, noise – and odd recent occurrences like a new owner taking his foal home on a bus! Back in 1656, West Ardsley residents unsuccessfully petitioned to abolish the fair as a social nuisance. Nowadays it is reduced to 24 August and 17 September, with a strong Romany presence.

The oldest agricultural building in Yorkshire is believed to be the Whiston Memorial Barn, near Rotherham, dating from the thirteenth century. It had two threshing floors, and stored grain – with due tax, of course – for the medieval serfs of the lords of the manor. The barn has recently been restored as the village hall.

The early seventeenth-century Wortley Top Forge is the oldest heavy iron forge in the world. (*See* 'Industrial Revolution' forerunners.)

England's first known duck decoy, 1657, was at Potteric Carr, a boggy fen just south-east of Doncaster, favoured by wildfowl. Nowadays it is a 200-hectare nature reserve under the Yorkshire Wildlife Trust.

Created by Act of Parliament in 1758, the Middleton Railway carried coal by wagonway horses from the pit to Leeds factories; and from 1812 its steam locomotive,

Octagonal chapel, Heptonstall.

built by Matthew Murray, was the first to be commercially successful – all of which pre-dated George Stephenson's achievements.

The oldest Methodist chapel (1764) still used is the beautiful octagonal building at Heptonstall.

The Wharfedale Agricultural Show, held annually in May at Otley, is England's oldest (1796).

The year 1891 saw the earliest electric tram-car commuting between Roundhay Park and Sheepscar, Leeds.

Shipley Glen Cable Railway is the oldest cable-hauled tramway in Great Britain, built in 1895.

The first Carnegie library was built in Keighley in 1904.

Bradford's first trolley-bus service began on 20 June 1911. Bradford was also the last city to keep its trolley-buses.

OLIVER'S DIARY

The Revd Oliver Heywood (1630-1702), ejected from his Northowram chapel in 1662, seemed to delight in noting scurrilous behaviour – cockfighting, profanity, drink, immorality. He was particularly disturbed by an alehouse situated between Halifax and Bradford whose sign showed a naked couple 'in a shameful manner'. A sign of the times, no doubt… Puritanism giving way to Restoration mores.

'ON ILKLA MOOR BAHT 'AT'

The story behind the Yorkshire Anthem, which starts, 'Tha's been a-courtin', Mary Jane,' involves a hymn tune, 'Cranbrook', curiously penned about 1805 by Thomas Clark, a Methodist choir conductor from Canterbury (aye, a Southerner!). As for the words, on some choir outing, possibly from Halifax around 1860, traversing Ilkley Moor, this young man had lost his hat whilst paying court to Mary Jane. After telling off the lad, moaning that he'd get his death of cold and be buried, his mother (or whoever) takes the tale forward through the food chain – worms, ducks, people – 'then we shall all have etten thee!' A sad tale, but sung with gusto across God's Own Country.

'ONWARD CHRISTIAN SOLDIERS'

The hymn was specially composed by the Revd Sabine Baring Gould (1834-1924) for a Whitsuntide treat at Horbury, where he had been appointed in 1864. He used music already composed by Sir Arthur Sullivan.

After despatching her to a vicarage in York to learn some social graces, the author wed a young mill girl, Grace Taylor. He was warned by a parishioner that Grace might not be careful enough in spending his money, earning the reply, 'I don't want a woman to spend my money. I want a woman who will save it.' Anyway, they wed in Wakefield, spawning fifteen children.

As a folklorist SPG collected country songs, deleting rude words as necessary. He claimed to have traced back the nursery rhyme Jack and Jill to a Scandinavian myth in which the two children were kidnapped by the moon; and every full moon they can still be seen, carrying a full bucket on a pole.

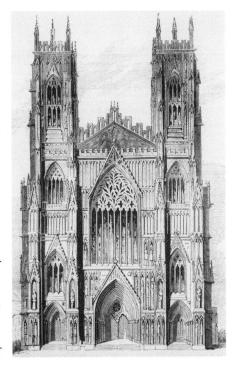

The west front of York Minster, which was set on fire by Jonathon Martin.

An intriguing work is *Yorkshire Oddities*, with examples of folk like the York Minster arsonist, Jonathan Martin. But SPG was an odd bod himself. He often wrote standing up. And he was apt to recruit choir boys by strong-arm methods. At a children's party he reputedly asked one child, ' And whose little girl are you?' A tearful Joan eventually replied, 'Yours, Daddy!'

OXENHOPE STRAW RACE

In an otherwise quiet village just south of Haworth, this charity event, held in early July, first started in 1975. Generally the teams, mostly in fancy dress, and attracted from a wide area, run or saunter in pairs, often with horseplay and badinage, and carrying bales of straw. Beginning late morning at the Waggon and Horses they call at five pubs, one member drinking a pint in each, run downhill into the village centre where the bales are picked up outside the Bay Horse; proceed down the valley and up to the Dog and Gun – some three miles altogether. Some serious athletes reckon to cover it in about seventeen minutes.

PACE EGGING

'Pace' derives from *pasch,* meaning Easter. In memory of the stone rolled from Christ's tomb, this is the season when children rolled their pace eggs down a slope. The eggs are, of course, hard-boiled and coloured with a pinch of coffee, polish, onion skin, etc. In West Yorkshire some youngsters like to 'jarp' another's egg, by knocking it with the sharper end of their own, the object being to crack the opponent's without suffering oneself. Since 1980 jarping competitions have taken place at Cusworth Hall Museum.

On Good Friday in Weavers Square, Heptonstall, hundreds of spectators congregate, sustained by hot cross buns, to watch the lively Pace Egging Play – an ancient mumming theme of good versus evil, death and renewal. St George crosses swords with various opponents – the Bold Slasher, the King of Egypt, the Black Prince of Paradise, Hector; and as each succumbs (with astonishing acrobatics on the hard surface) revivals are carried out by the Doctor with his panacea flagon. Lots of encouragement is given by the dashing, if dishevelled, Tosspot. Allowing for intervals spent by the actors in the adjacent pub, there are four performances, each enriched with some admirable *ad libs,*

Oxenhope Straw Race.

Pace egging play,
Heptonstall: the Black
Prince of Paradise
challenges St George.

prompted by a good-humoured crowd which gives generously to the collection for various charities.

A variation of death and revival is given by the Grenoside (Sheffield) Longsword Dancers on Boxing Day when their performance outside the Old Harrow Inn culminates with the symbolic beheading of their captain. A compelling sword-lock is placed over his head, but he lives on – foretelling that the New Year will shortly replace the old.

PACKHORSES

In upland areas unsuitable for wheeled vehicles, teams generally rode in single file behind a leader known as the Jagger (after the German Jaeger ponies) whose horse carried bells to warn oncoming traffic. Canvas or leather panniers strapped on either side carried such goods as wool, coal, charcoal, peat, hides, corn and metal. Occasionally ladies who rode pillion were charged as half a pack! Salt was an important commodity both for preserving meat and for use in textile dyeing. It had to be carried from the Northwich area, Cheshire, over the moors from Woodhead and Saltersbrook for south Yorkshire. Psalter Lane, Sheffield is a reminder of one destination.

Traders known as 'broggers' conveyed wool from outlying farms to clothiers in Halifax. The Long Causeway was a partially paved track from Halifax to Luddenden and Hebden Bridge, where there remains a fine stone packhorse bridge (built in around 1510) through to Burnley. These bridges had narrow arches to allow single file traffic, with low parapets for the panniers.

With the development of turnpike roads and canals, packhorses became redundant. Exhibits at the Bankfield Museum, Halifax include pack saddles and bell collars.

PANCAKE BELL

In many parish churches (Bingley, Penistone, Batley) the ringing of the Pancake Bell at 11 a.m. on Shrove Tuesday was the signal for housewives to get cooking. Originally the bell called parishioners to church for shriving (i.e. forgiveness) prior to Lent. So on this last day before Lent the kitchen fats were used to cook pancakes. With Ash Wednesday the Lenten fast started – or so the theory ran.

PARTY PROMPT

When, in 1785, the Revd Dr Edmund Cartwright (1743-1823), former Professor of Poetry, Oxford, attended a party of cotton manufacturers, he learned that the weavers couldn't keep pace with spinning production. Accordingly, helped by a joiner and blacksmith, he invented a power loom, which helped to inaugurate the factory era. His first model did not catch on immediately, but with refinements he set up a weaving factory in Hallgate West, Doncaster. Success came with a substantial Manchester

Packhorse Bridge, Hebden Bridge.

order. Local weavers, however, were unimpressed. The factory was burnt and looms were smashed. The following year, 1793, when his business collapsed, Cartwright left Doncaster and applied himself to other technical projects. The Cartwright Memorial Hall in Bradford was completed in 1904.

PEEL

Bradford actually erected its first statue to a Lancastrian! And it was splendidly deserved, too. Sir Robert (1788-1850) was famous for founding the Metropolitan Police Force in 1829; the Mines Act, 1842, forbidding the employment of women and children in mines; the 1844 Factory Act, limiting the working hours of women and children; and the Repeal of the Corn Laws, 1846, leading to freer trade and better times. The Corn Laws, imposed in 1815, had forbidden the importation of foreign corn until the price of home-grown wheat rose to 80s a quarter, benefiting farmers but starving the poor. Sculpted by William Behnes, the bronze figure holds a Parliamentary Bill. Originally it stood in Peel Place, unveiled on 6 November 1855, a public holiday. It has been re-sited in Peel Park, Bolton Road.

PENANCE

In May 1705, Sarah Lister, barefooted, head bowed, clad in a white sheet and carrying a white wand, walked slowly down the aisle in Royston church. She was directed to stand before the pulpit. There, to the enlarged congregation, she admitted and repented of her fornication with Robert Shillitoe. Some of these acts of public humiliation, sanctioned by ecclesiastical courts, lasted until the nineteenth century.

PERAMBULATIONS

Beating the bounds, or 'Rammalations', walking the parish boundaries, was customarily done at Rogationtide, before Ascension Day. It was done partly to re-assert the community's rights as to who owned what and partly to initiate children into their future rights. A certain amount of horseplay (a measured push into a ditch, or a bounce on a stone) might emphasise a particular feature – beck, hedge, pathway etc. Refreshments provided by church or parish were much looked forward to after this healthy ritual. It still happens in some villages (e.g. at Shelley, on New Year's Day).

PEW RENTS

For centuries pew rents ensured part of a church's income. But the principle was often controversial, and without warrant in Holy Scripture. Social snobbery was endorsed, with the more expensive seats at the front or in the centre nave. A further argument was that poor parishioners were sidelined and discouraged, some turning to the more democratic seating arrangement in nonconformist chapels. A reminder of these times is a brass plate on pew door in Otley church, proclaiming 'John Bolton's pew, 1789'. Rents survived here till 1865.

WILFRED PICKLES (1904-78)

This genial communicator, a Halifax lad, made his name in the homely radio programme, *Have a Go*. He and his wife, Mabel, visited a different location each week and interviewed ordinary folk; these told their own stories before trying their luck at a quiz for cash. Such questions as 'Are yer courtin'?' might be put to anyone, even unlikely elderly guests, whose answers so often resulted in 'Give 'em the money, Barney' (producer Barney Colehan). This family institution was enjoyed by twenty million listeners and lasted for twenty-one years. Later Violet Carson at the piano was to become the no-nonsense Ena Sharples, she of the permanent hairnet, in the early days of *Coronation Street*.

Wilfred was the first BBC news reader with a marked regional accent. Often he would add a pithy Yorkshire comment before his usual farewell – 'and to all in the North, good neet!' He was transferred to London in 1942 in the hope that his West Riding accent might confuse the Germans. Eventually he moved on to ENSA tours, and the West End stage. He was awarded an OBE in 1950.

PIECE HALL, HALIFAX

During the second half of the eighteenth century cloth halls became a feature of the Pennine textile trade (Penistone in 1763, Huddersfield in 1766, Bradford in 1773, Leeds in 1775). Designed by Thomas Bradley, the Piece Hall opened on 1 January 1779 to receive woollen and worsted 'pieces' (about 30 yards long) made by handloom weavers in their cottages. Built around an open square were colonnaded stone-walled galleries divided into 315 rooms where pieces were stored. In the early days trading was confined to 10 a.m. until noon on Saturdays, with fines for defaults.

The Hall was severely functional and architecturally plain, Georgian without any attempt at contemporary embellishment. It had its critics, like Charles Dibdin (1788): '…it gave me the idea of a bee-hive: the prodigious number of cells, and the workers coming in and out with their bundles of cloth were exactly the loaded bees.'

This hyper-activity was not to last long. Increased mass production from factories and mills, and the development of warehouses, progressively reduced the opportunities for handloom weavers.

From about 1815 the Hall declined, becoming in 1871 a market for fish, fruit and vegetables. Saved from demolition in 1972 by one town council vote, it was restored and reopened four years later. Modern shoppers look for paintings, antiques, clothes, models, books, etc. The Hall regularly hosts markets and festivals.

PILGRIMAGE OF GRACE

This was a rising mainly against Henry VIII's suppression of the monasteries and his declaration of himself as Supreme Head of the Church of England. Beginning in Lincolnshire in October of 1536, the rising spread to Yorkshire under the leadership of Robert Aske, an East Riding lawyer; marching westwards the rebels reached Ackworth, and captured Pontefract Castle. Thomas Howard, Duke of Norfolk, was sent to parley at Doncaster Bridge, and the 30,000 rebels abandoned their mission after assurances were given to consider further the restoration of the Catholic religion, and

Piece Hall, Halifax.

the removal of Thomas Cromwell, Vicar-General. When nothing happened there were further disturbances. The peasants feared betrayal. In Leeds parish church appeared a notice – 'Commons, keep well your harness, trust no gentleman'. Some fears were justified. Henry invited the leaders to London to discuss terms, but arrested them. Over 200 followers were executed. Aske and Nicholas Tempest of Ackworth were hanged in York.

Suppression of the monasteries continued, St Oswald's Priory at Nostell in the heartland of the rebellion surrendering in 1540.

PLOT NAYT

Otherwise Bonfire Night, when the Gunpowder Plot was commemorated with garden as well as street bonfires, and small boys swarmed everywhere to 'chump' (collect) anything combustible. Bigger lads might go 'progging', or foraging in a neighbouring bonfire for desirable bits. Eating parkin pigs and treacle toffee was also keenly anticipated. Guy Fawkes had been a York lad, schooled at St Peter's – which doesn't do bonfires!

PLOUGH STOTS

On Plough Monday, the first after 6 January (Epiphany), plough stots (jacks or lads, according to district) dragged a decorated plough through the village, begging money for drink. If this was not forthcoming a retributive strip might be ploughed across their front garden. Originally stots were bullocks drawing the plough, but the name came to be applied to the young men. In Victorian times, young men at Altofts attired in long be-ribboned smocks blew on large horns and called out 'largess, largess'. In Edwardian times at Ecclesfield 'plough bullocks' in long white smocks and top hats hauled the plough, a lad with pig's bladder on a stick pretending to beat them. Sometimes they devised a rough-and-tumble play.

PLUG RIOTS AND PETITIONS

Chartism was a working-class movement aiming at such reforms as the election of working class MPs and secret ballots. Petitions were drawn up to present to Parliament. Militancy followed the rejection in 1842 of the second petition bearing over 3 million signatures. Five thousand men marched on Cleckheaton mills to draw plugs from steam boilers, rendering them useless. On 12 August, 20,000 men marched on Todmorden, and the next day on Halifax, urging mill closures and support. Troops moved into the streets of Halifax.

One curious reprisal against a farmer was the stripping bare of a field of turnips at Thornhill Lees.

Although the third great petition failed in 1848, enormous publicity had been won for the cause by Feargus O'Connor, who in 1837 had launched the *Northern Star* newspaper in Leeds; ten years later he was elected as MP for Nottingham.

POACHER PAGE

During the 1850s Ann Page was a notorious poacher around Horsforth. Of manly attitude and appearance, she grew a beard – and owned two ferocious bulldogs.

POLLUTION

Every age and seemingly every place has a different environmental problem. A Thorner Court Roll of 1549 ruled, 'No-one must wash any linen cloth or flax in the spring called Saint Sithe Well… or put in anything rotten, on pain of 4*d* fine'.

But worse conditions were to come. A River Pollution Commission of 1860 condemned Bradford Canal Basin as … 'so corrupt that large volumes of inflammable gases were given off, this at times forming the amusement of local boys who would set the canal on fire, the flames rising six feet high and running along the surface of the water for many yards, engulfing boats'.

PONTE FIRST

The Pontefract by-election of 1872 was the first occasion for the use of the newly enacted secret ballot.

POST OFFICE PROGRESS?

'On Sundays, Good Friday and Christmas Day the chief office is open until 10 a.m. only. On week days the office is closed at 9 p.m. but the box is open all night. There are four deliveries of letters etc at 7 and 10.30 a.m., and at 2.30 and 7.30 p.m.' (*Re* Priory Place Post Office, Doncaster from *Slater's Directory*, Part 2, 1887.)

POUND

Especially before enclosures, straying animals often caused problems and even damage. A pinder appointed by the manor court had the job of rounding them up and impounding them. Then, as now, villagers were often reluctant to pay fines, and pounds, or pinfolds, were broken into. At Ossett in 1327 Alice de Heton was fined 12d for allowing her cows to stray and then illegally freeing them. At Tadcaster in 1590 Edmund Remynton was fined by the manor court for making a 'rescue'.

There are some survivors – Hooten Pagnell has a cattle pound. While the pinfold at Barnby Dun, near Doncaster, has been made into a neat public garden, Fishlake's, near Thorne, though less well kept, looks more authentic. This village had a pinder until 1929. His salary came partly from charges made for grazing rights on roadside verges.

PRATTY FLOWERS

Both Huddersfield and Holmfirth claim it as their anthem – but Holmfirth seems to have a prior and stronger case! It is the centrepiece of the Feast Sing on the Sunday before Whitsunday. As a folk ballad, its provenance may lie in eighteenth-century London gardens, but around 1850 it was adapted with beautiful harmonies by Joe Perkins, conductor of the Choral Society. The theme is of a lovesick girl, lamenting

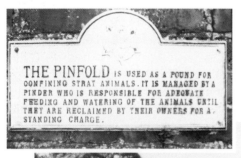

Fishlake Pinfold.

THE PINFOLD IS USED AS A POUND FOR CONFINING STRAY ANIMALS. IT IS MANAGED BY A PINDER WHO IS RESPONSIBLE FOR ADEQUATE FEEDING AND WATERING OF THE ANIMALS UNTIL THEY ARE RECLAIMED BY THEIR OWNERS FOR A STANDING CHARGE.

Pro-American Arches, Aberford.

for her shepherd swain gone to fight the French and Spaniards, but reconciled to the consolations of 'yon green gardens where those pratty flowers grow'. She thinks hopefully of their wedding on his return.

PRO-AMERICAN ARCHES

Parlington Drive, Aberford leads to a pleasant parkland walk at the end of which stands a triple Triumphal Arch inscribed 'Liberty In North America Triumphant MDCCLXXXIII' (i.e. 1783, commemorating the end of the American War of Independence). This impressive folly was designed by Thomas Leverton for Sir Thomas Gascoigne MP – a manifest supporter of the American cause.

PROPHET JOHN WROE (1782-1863)

Born at Bowling, Bradford Wroe became a religious fanatic, forming a Christian Israelite Sect, growing a long white beard and riding on a donkey. This deluded trickster displayed posters announcing that he would walk on the River Aire at Apperley Bridge on 29 February 1824.

Thousands came, but finding they had to pay to enter, soon grew restless, despite the hired brass band. The afternoon was cold and sunless when the prophet ventured a few tentative steps, but as the chilly waters failed to part, he was pelted with missiles, some disappointed onlookers shouting 'Drown him!' Friends led him away to ribald shouts.

Subsequently he drew attention to fasting on nuts and berries, and, such was his charisma, he persuaded gullible followers to fund a 'mission' – which foundered with accusations regarding the treatment of young girls, and resulted in a ducking in a Pudsey pond. When he sold 'House of Israel' rings to followers, some of their fingers turned green. Even so, they built him a mansion at Wrenthorpe.

Wroe travelled widely in Europe and America, dying at Fitzroy, Australia, despite claims of immortality.

PUBS

Among scores of our interesting pubs are the following:

The Old Silent Inn, Stanbury, where Bonnie Prince Charlie hid for a time while on the run; the locals kept quiet.

The Old Cock Inn, Halifax, where the Halifax Permanent Building Society was formed in 1852.

Up to 1839 the Black Bull Inn, Kirkgate, Birstall, had an upstairs room used as a court. The magistrates' chair and prisoner's box remain.

PUSH UP!

Such are the gradients between Bradford and Queensbury that Leeds–Rochdale coach passengers sometimes had to get out and push. Standing 1150ft above sea level, Queensbury was once Causewayend, the very name suggesting packhorse times.

QUAGGA

Exhibited occasionally in Doncaster Museum is a quagga foal – a hybrid, part zebra, part donkey. The name originated in the Hottentot language of South Africa in around 1785. The animal is of some antiquity, and was preserved by a Scots taxidermist, Dr Hugh Reid, about 1830. How it turned up in Doncaster is something of a mystery. Dr Reid may have brought it from Owston Park or Nostell Priory.

QUEENLY INDISCRETIONS

Before her royal wedding, Catherine Howard, high-spirited fifth bride of Henry VIII, had had an affair with Francis Dereham, and was unwise enough to appoint him as her secretary. During August 1541, while Henry was visiting Bretton Hall, she indiscreetly entertained Thomas Culpepper in her rooms at Pontefract Castle. One of her ladies-in-waiting, Lady Rochford, kept cave, making sure the Queen's doors were locked from the inside. But tongues wagged.

Further to an inquiry at Doncaster, and the torture of Dereham and Culpepper, Catherine admitted adultery, and on 13 February 1542 she and Lady Rochford were beheaded at the Tower of London, on the same spot as Anne Boleyn had met her fate.

QUEEN OF SONG

Daughter of a Brighouse gardener, Miss Susan Sykes (1819-1905), later Mrs Sunderland, worked as a mill girl, but had no formal training as a soprano. She reputedly learnt rhythmic phrases with the unusual aid of blacksmith Luke Settle beating time on his anvil. Walking miles to engagements in her early singing years, she quickly won fame.

At the 1858 Leeds Musical Festival, Queen Victoria was sufficiently impressed to tell her, 'I am the Queen of England but you are the Queen of Song'. Mrs Sunderland sang at venues through the UK, including Buckingham Palace, retiring in 1864.

The Mrs Sunderland Musical Competition, begun in 1889, remains a major regional event held annually in Huddersfield Town Hall.

QUICK CHANGES

Now and again circumstances dictate a rapid re-orientation of usage. At the outbreak of war in 1914, for instance, the Shambles at Wetherby stopped being a market and was adapted for use as a rifle range.

RACE RIVALRY

Stagecoaches had appeared in the later eighteenth century. Drawn by four horses, usually, the vehicle carried six passengers inside and up to twelve on the roof. A 'stage' was a hostelry where the horses were changed and passengers alighted to stretch their legs and seek refreshment. Coachmen were notoriously temperamental. William Bramley was often drunk while in charge of the 'Rockingham' to Leeds. Outside it might be freezing in winter; inside it could be stuffy, smelly and bumpy, given the state of the roads, which were poor, especially before turnpikes took over. York to London took four days.

Coach proprietors were competitive, and their drivers were instructed to hasten. In 1817 rival coaches from York, finding themselves nearing Leeds, applied their whips, with the result that the *True Briton*, trying to forge ahead, overturned after running inadvertently into a dung heap. There were bruised passengers, one woman losing several fingers.

ARTHUR RANSOME (1884-1967)

West Yorkshire has produced some astonishing folk who have led double lives. Many of us will have been captivated by *Swallows and Amazons* (1930), a children's holiday adventure set in the Lake District and Norfolk, with lots of camping, sailing and fishing. The author had had an indifferent boyhood at Rugby School, and later at the Yorkshire College. Step by modest step, he did better as a London journalist, though a controversial book on Oscar Wilde brought notoriety and a lawsuit which, happily, he won. He became interested in Russia and worked as foreign correspondent for the *Daily News*. Meeting the Revolutionary leaders Lenin and Trotsky, he conducted an affair with Evgenia Shelepina, the latter's secretary, gaining valuable information, and eventually marrying her after a divorce from his first wife. Under his code name S76 he passed information concerning the Revolution to MI6. He was suspected and later cleared of being a double agent.

Ransome went on to write for the *Guardian*, especially the *Country Diary*. An eventful career indeed! It just goes to show the truth of that saying, 'Niver trust a stranger till tha's wintered and summered 'im – aye, an' wintered 'im again' … especially, one might add, if he was born into a middle-class family in Hyde Park, Leeds.

RECORDS

Born at Horsforth, Foster Powell in 1733 walked to London from York, and back, in five days and eighteen hours, a feat he several times repeated, the last time at the age of fifty-eight. He made a modest amount by betting on himself, yet despised wealth. He died in 1793.

On 29 October 1864 at the Bradford City Sporting Ground thirty-two year old Elizabeth Sharp completed a 1,000 mile walk that had lasted six weeks. A brass band helped to celebrate her triumph.

According to the *Guinness Book of World Records* the biggest onion ever, weighing in at 10lb 14oz (4.9kg) was grown in 1990 by Vincent Throup of Silsden.

Sir Leonard Hutton (1916-90) still holds the record for the highest test innings (364) by an Englishman. This was at the Oval against Australia in August 1938, when he batted for thirteen hours and seventeen minutes. Born at Fulneck, Len played first for Pudsey St Lawrence, and was the first professional to captain England (1952-5). In a wonderful career he made 40,140 runs at an average of 55.41.

Emley Moor Transmitting Station, near Huddersfield, stands at 1084ft, the UK's tallest structure. It was completed in 1970.

The 900 acres surrounding Temple Newsam, Leeds constitute one of Europe's largest urban parks.

RHUBARB TRIANGLE

Imported into England, probably from Italy, during the Middle Ages, rhubarb was used for medicinal purposes like 'cramps and convulsions'. During the nineteenth century it became a speciality in the Dewsbury/Morley-Wakefield area. Generations of miners used night soil in its production. Commercial cultivation had so advanced by the 1870s that trainloads were sent to Covent Garden. Wakefield holds a Rhubarb Festival in February.

RIDING THE STANG

Sometimes there was collective village action against an erring or violent husband. Young men would tie his effigy onto a stee (ladder or stang), mount it on a cart and trail it to the malefactor's house, accompanied by much 'rough music' from pots, pans, whistles, gongs, etc. On arrival the stang leader shouted an indictment to a well-rehearsed formula. Threats were issued and echoed. The action was repeated on the two following nights. On the third occasion the effigy was burnt.

The effects were probably salutary in many cases. Sometimes the family, humiliated, left the district. But in Leeds, in 1667, one miscreant thus treated fired a shotgun into the crowd, killing two.

RINGING ADAM BELLS

These social occasions were held around the Huddersfield and Holme Valley areas in later Victorian times. After a few drinks at a family party or wedding, volunteers sat on the floor in circles, men on the inside, women on the outer, to sing risque songs, with increasing rocking movements until several fell over. Measured female immodesty led to great hilarity… and sometimes familiarity.

RIOTS

The later eighteenth century was a riotous age in West Yorkshire, with soldiers frequently deployed in the streets. In April 1740 food shortages in Wakefield brought a corn riot lasting four days, all due to attempts to secure flour. Mills were damaged at Dewsbury and Thornhill.

During July 1781 violent protests broke out against enclosures at Stannington and Hallam.

In disturbances at Beeston, Leeds, in 1797, a cloth mill was destroyed. While these examples could be readily multiplied, there were serious problems in other areas (Wales, London, the Midlands…).

RIVE-KITE SUNDAY

Just after Martinmas (late November), with the imminent departure of recently hired young farm lads and servant girls, a gargantuan meal was laid on at home for their last Sunday. 'Rive-kite' means split stomach! Almost a year later, if the young person wanted a change of job, the last working day was Pack Rag Day when he gathered together all his possessions.

ROBIN HOOD

History offers many hints and alternatives. A Robin Hod supposedly fled from justice at York in 1225, while a fourteenth-century Court Roll at Wakefield mentions Robert Hode and wife, Matilda, outlawed for being a follower of the rebel Thomas of Lancaster.

Was it really in Barnsdale Forest, near Doncaster, where Robin and his outlaws, dressed as shepherds, baited the unpopular Bishop of Hereford, forcing him to a venison dinner and charging him £300, before obliging him to dance till exhausted? The well at Burghwallis marks a supposed likely area.

Kirklees Hall, near Brighouse, has one traditional grave from the mid-thirteenth century. This legend claims that Robin, as an old man, sought shelter at the priory, where a nun — coincidentally a cousin? — bled him, maybe over-zealously. He blew his horn, fired his last arrow, and instructed Little John to bury him where it landed.

The name is perpetuated in the Robin Hood Airport near Doncaster.

ROOM ON TOP

The Leeds-Manchester railway proved very popular, as the *Wakefield Journal* made clear soon after the opening in 1839: 'At Hebden Bridge so many people boarded the train that they climbed onto the roof and had to stand as there were so many up there.'

ROYAL TOUCH

'Given to a woman of Sandal to help her on a journey to the king "for a touch" 5s.' (All Saints church parish vestry book, 1685, Cawthorne). Until the practice was stopped by George I it was believed that the sovereign, appointed by God, could cure diseases, notably scrofula, 'the king's evil'. Royal treatment included the gift of a coin. Charles II reputedly cured many thousands of his subjects.

RUSH BEARING

This old-time early September festival was revived at Sowerby Bridge for the 1977 Silver Jubilee, and takes place on a Saturday and Sunday. Bundles of plaited rushes are attractively arranged to form a pyramid, and mounted on a two-wheeled cart drawn by about sixty men in panama hats, white shirts, black trousers and clogs. A daring maiden perches on top. The procession is accompanied by a brass band, morris dancers, mummers, and en route are street entertainment, markets and exhibitions. The route may vary from year to year, but generally sets off on the Saturday from St John's church and proceeds to the Canal Basin; and on the Sunday starts from St Peter's church, Sowerby, following a circuitous itinerary likely to involve a stop at

Sowerby Bridge
rushbearers.

Cottonstones church, before winding up for a blessing at St Bartholomew's church, Ripponden.

The festival recalls times when fresh rushes were placed on stone or even earthen floors of churches, providing a covering, some degree of warmth and muffling sound. The need to replace the rushes gave rise to ceremony and festival. In the seventeenth century, despite the religious basis, the proceedings used to be rowdy, occasionally with fisticuffs. In Leeds, 1615, followers of the Revd Alexander Cooke, who hated the festival, smashed musicians' instruments, provoking anger, threats, and a report to the Star Chamber. The Revd Oliver Heywood in 1680 reported 'many outrages' at Haworth, 'in revellings and rantings'.

Odd tales accrue. An old superstition claimed that a woman touching the rushcart might soon become pregnant! New-laid rushes brought insects, so hedgehogs were introduced to keep them down.

SALE OF A TOWN

In 1824 William George Spencer Cavendish, 6th Duke of Devonshire, was financially embarrassed. He wanted to pay off certain gambling debts and to finance work at Chatsworth. Accordingly, except for one house, he sold Wetherby. Properties under the hammer included 200 dwellings, two posting houses and a corn mill. The Swan and Talbot inn went for £1,500; the Crown, Red Lion and Blue Boar together realised £2,870. Altogether the sale made £168, 561.

SALES OF WIVES

The *Doncaster Gazette* of 25 March 1803 reported that a local man had sold his wife for one guinea to a butcher in Sheffield market. She went to her new master with a halter round her neck.

In 1826, at Emley market cross, John Turton sold his wife Mary for two half-crowns to William Kaye of Scisset. After W.K.'s death she went back to Turton for another thirty years.

In 1858 Hartley Thompson auctioned his wife in a beer shop at Little Horton, Bradford, the proceedings having been previously publicised by a bellman.

But such sales were not unique to Yorkshire, as Thomas Hardy's novel *The Mayor of Casterbridge* shows.

SALTAIRE

This present-day World Heritage Site was the creation of philanthropic mill-owner Sir Titus Salt (1803-1876) who dealt in wool, cotton, silk and especially alpaca, with which he had experimented since 1836, especially after Queen Victoria had shown interest.

He may have been prompted by Disraeli's novel *Sybil* (1847), in which Trafford's Mill had a good reputation. He was well aware also of Edward Akroyd's model village and mill (1849) at Copley.

So in 1851, Great Exhibition year, with architects Lockwood and Mawson, he began to plan Saltaire. Some of the streets were named after family members – Titus, Caroline (his wife), plus Shirley, Jane, Mary, Constance, Helen, Ada, Fanny, Amelia, Herbert, William Henry, Edward and George – plus, of course, Victoria Road and Albert Road. A model village of 823 solid houses was built for the 4,500 workers at the new Salt's Mill, with baths, almshouses, hospital, school, library, a Congregational church, and a park – for which he imposed strict rules of behaviour, including a ban on music, public meetings, bad language, gambling and use of the playgrounds on Sundays. Sir Titus tolerated no pub, no pawnbroker, no police station! Club and Institute were 'to supply the advantages of a public house without its evils'.

The mill was once the largest workroom in the world – 60,000 square ft. A hard worker himself, he was a stickler for efficiency. As in other workplaces late workers were fined. But employees enjoyed trips to the countryside (the Dales, especially) and the seaside. Other firms eventually imitated these initiatives.

One view of Saltaire was that it was clean, healthy and orderly, presenting a happier face of capitalism. Some dismissed Salt as a sanctimonious old tyrant. John Ruskin thought that he was too paternalistic, bent on subordinating his captive workforce.

Of his 1874 statue, placed in front of the Bradford Town Hall, Sir Titus remarked, 'I see you have made me a pillar of salt'. In 1896 the monument was transferred to Lister Park. Another statue stands in Robert's Park, Saltaire. His funeral witnessed one of Yorkshire's huge turn-outs with an estimated 100,000 mourners lining the streets between Bradford and Saltaire.

But even great things change. Trade suffered, and in the 1890s the mill was taken over by a local business consortium, to be revamped again in the 1970s by Jonathon

Silver, and becoming a World Heritage Site in 2002. Nowadays the mill's variety of shops sell textiles, arts and crafts, gifts, antiques, books, furniture, domestic items; there is also a permanent exhibition of the pictures of Bradford-born David Hockney.

SANCTUARY KNOCKER

Until 2002 St John the Baptist church, Adel had a highly decorative bronze sanctuary ring, or door knocker, cast in York in around 1200. Sadly it was stolen, though the replica is a satisfying work of art. It shows a man-eating monster. Or is the victim being disgorged? Presumably it illustrates the power of the church in saving him from hell. In times past a couple too poor to buy a wedding ring held the sanctuary ring as they made their vows.

In medieval times a fugitive actually reaching it could claim right of sanctuary within the church for up to forty days, until his fate was decided. He might then be escorted to a port. King James I abolished this right in 1623.

SCHOOL RULES

'Every afternoon the Girls' School will be devoted to plain Needlework and Knitting. Parents will be allowed to send their own or their Children's Clothes to be made on Wednesdays, Thursdays and Fridays.' (Cantley National Schools, Doncaster, late Victorian times.)

At Rotherham High School for Girls in the Edwardian era there were many restrictions, not least at dinner time. Silence was enjoined at various stages, while, for instance, plates were being passed to the head of the table. Moreover, 'if any water is spilt, a fine of 1d must be paid by all the girls concerned to the Second Mistress'.

SCOTS INVADERS

After repulsing the English at Bannockburn the Scots made a series of invasions deep into northern England. In 1318 they reached Wetherby, with much burning and killing. King Edward II had other problems. Barons, led by Thomas of Lancaster, were protesting at his favourites (Piers Gaveston and Hugh Despenser); despite support from Scotland, a rebellion resulted in the rebels' defeat at Boroughbridge in 1322, and the execution of Lancaster at Pontefract.

Scott Lane in Wetherby may (or may not) recall the old looting tradition. More likely its origins lie in the later enterprise of Scots drovers bringing their herds to more southerly markets, especially London. There must have been colourful scenes with Scots pipers leading straggling trails of animals controlled by men and dogs. At Skipton blacksmiths replaced shoes for cattle – two for each cloven hoof. Another stopping place was Ferrybridge on the Great North Road, where the drovers stayed at inns like the Greyhound. The trade ended with the coming of the railways in the 1840s.

SCOUT HALL

Situated on the Shibden estate, Halifax, this derelict building, uninhabited since the 1980s, was built in 1681 for John Mitchell, a silk importer. It is remarkable for its calendar arrangements – 365 window panes, 52 rooms and 12 doors.

Salt's Mill, Saltaire.

Sir Titus Salt.   Sanctuary knocker, St John's Church, Adel.

Scott Lane plaque, Wetherby.

SCROGGLING THE HOLLY

At Haworth on a mid-November Sunday afternoon a procession of children in Victorian costume follow a band and Morris Men up the cobbled Main Street to the parish church of St Michael and All Angels. There, on the churchyard steps, the young Holly Queen is crowned and symbolically unlocks the gates so the Christmas Spirit can circulate. 'Scroggling' is a local word meaning gathering.

SCRAMBLING

There have been many instances of seasonal benevolence by authority figures towards children. A former May Day custom at Ermysted School, Skipton was for the boys to strew flowers on the steps of the master's house and the classroom floor, the master responding by throwing handfuls of coins in the air.

Even a few mill owners took part. At 12 noon on Shrove Tuesday, the gaffer of Meltham Mills near Netherton strode into the yard, and showered bags of pennies towards the assembled and excited youngsters.

SHEFFIELD CAROLS

Massed carol singing was part of a tradition amongst South Yorkshire church folk from Victorian times. More recently the idea has grown in pubs west and north of Sheffield, as far out as Penistone and Stocksbridge (for example, at the Travellers Rest, Oughtibridge; the Royal Hotel, Dungworth; the Crown and Glove, Stannington; the Blue Ball, Worrall). Scores of singers roar out traditional and local carols – some amusing ones, with robust choruses, and all of which makes for exhilarating evenings and Sunday lunchtimes during the latter part of November and through till Christmas.

SHEFFIELD OUTRAGES

Sheffield had a considerable history of violent protest, whether in food riots, disappointment following the 1832 Reform Act (which had enfranchised only the middle classes) or the Chartist disturbances in the 1840s. In 1867-8 the term 'rattening' became widespread: it meant pressure by unions (e.g. the cutlery industry and the saw-grinding fraternity) on non-union labour to join, and there were thefts of their tools and threatening letters sent. Non-union members suffered gunpowder attacks. Elisha Parker of Dore was shot at; gunpowder was strewn near his home; and some of his work 'rattened' (i.e. sabotaged).

Further to a hostile press and offended public opinion, a Special Commission of Inquiry granted immunity to anyone ready to testify. William Broadhead, Secretary of the Sawgrinders Union, and landlord of the Royal George, admitted having paid two men to murder an employer thought to have too many apprentices.

A Royal Commission into trade unions led in 1871 to their protection, but with a tightening of the criminal law in terms of intimidation and molestation. Legalisation of unions followed in 1873.

Twenty years earlier a Sheffield physician, Dr Knight, had drawn public attention to the unwholesome working conditions of local grinders. Work done with a dry stone often entailed an early death from consumption and asthma, with an average life expectancy of thirty-five years. Wet grinders could hope for ten years more. He added wryly, 'I can convey some idea of the injuriousness of this occupation only by asserting that the hardest drinkers among the grinders are the longest lived among them, because they are longest and oftenest absent from their work'.

SHIBDEN LESBIAN

Anne Lister (1791-1840), a cultivated heiress of Shibden Hall, Halifax, managed to teach herself such arts as maths, Greek and music. She also kept a diary of local events, travel, gossip, religion, politics, relationships – and her feelings for some women. As a teenager at York's fashionable Manor School, she developed an intense affection for her roommate, Elizabeth Raine. A close liaison with Isabella Norcliffe of Langton Hall, near Malton, lasted for four years. Another ardent companion, Ann Walker went on holiday with her to Russia and they collaborated in investments in coal mining as

Scroggling the Holly procession, Haworth.

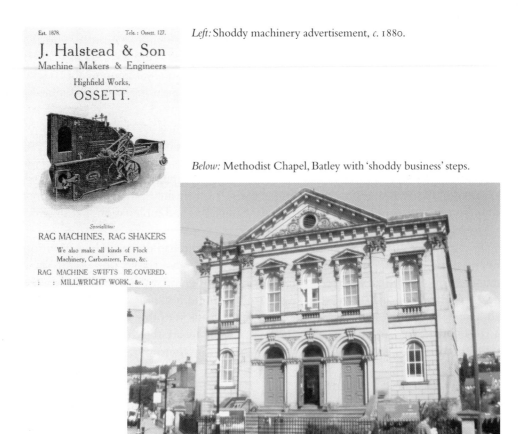

Est. 1878.   Tele.: Ossett. 127.

J. Halstead & Son
Machine Makers & Engineers

Highfield Works,
OSSETT.

Specialities:
RAG MACHINES, RAG SHAKERS
We also make all kinds of Flock
Machinery, Carbonizers, Fans, &c.
RAG MACHINE SWIFTS RE-COVERED.
: : MILLWRIGHT WORK, &c. : :

Left: Shoddy machinery advertisement, *c.* 1880.

Below: Methodist Chapel, Batley with 'shoddy business' steps.

well as the problems of running the Shibden estate. From another lover, Marianne, she caught VD, a diary entry of August 1821 detailing various potions taken to alleviate the condition. How much her genteel contemporaries in Halifax and York knew, or guessed, is speculative, but her frank independent outlook, entrepreneurial skills and flamboyance have made her an instructive study.

SHODDY

Recycling cloth from old rags worked with new wool meant that more blankets could be made cheaply. Inferior products could be consigned as burial blankets. The name 'shoddy' was unfortunate, coming to mean inferior. These renewals were started about 1813 by Benjamin Law (1773-1837), a Gomersal lad who became the Shoddy King; and who, incidentally, had two wives and seventeen children. The saying caught on, 'If it's got two ends we can spin it'. The Central Chapel, Batley (built 1869) became known as Shoddy Temple, due to business done by merchants on the steps after Sunday morning service.

Mungo practices were similar but involved recycled worsted, again with new wool added. This was started by George Parr, son of Ben Parr, Benjamin Law's brother-in-law... a tangled relationship in line with their trade. According to one story, George was determined this adaptation 'mun go' (i.e. must succeed). No effort was spared to make money. Even floor dust was sold as fertiliser.

SKELMANTHORPE FLAG

The village lies between Huddersfield and Barnsley. Its historic flag, designed in 1819 by a man called Bird, had quarters calling for Universal Suffrage, Justice, Liberty and the Brotherhood of Man. Its first appearance was at the Manchester Massacre in St Peter's Fields, 1819, when it heralded a demonstration at Almondbury Bank. It came out of hiding again at Wakefield in 1832 for the Reform Bill demonstrations; Chartist rallies in the 1840s; the end of the Crimean War, 1856, and the American Civil War, 1865.

SKIN OF A WITCH

Found guilty of poisoning for money, Mary Bateman, notorious swindler and poisoner, went to the scaffold at York on 20 March 1809. After dissection at Leeds General Infirmary her corpse was exhibited and bits of skin sold for a few coppers. Her skeleton is preserved in the Thackray Medical Museum, Leeds.

Skelmanthorpe flag.

The notorious Mary Bateman.

St Blaise, Bradford Wool Exchange.

STAR TURN

At St John's parish church, Halifax, a new John Snetzler organ was installed in 1766. The first organist to play a chosen piece (from the *Messiah*, in this case) was William Herschel, the future Astronomer Royal.

ST BLAISE'S FESTIVAL, BRADFORD

Blaise is the Patron Saint of wooolcombers: a wool comb was the instrument used in his martyrdom, AD 316. Bradford, as the woollen capital, once held septennial celebrations, the last on the 3 February 1825. All the various trades, decked in distinctive woollen apparel, and flourishing emblems, banners and fleeces, assembled at 8 a.m., with crowds already gathering. The immense procession included 24 woolstaplers, 38 spinners, 6 merchants, 56 apprentices, 160 woolsorters, 40 dyers, 30 combmakers and 470 woolcombers, led by bands from Bradford and Keighley, with macebearer, king, queen, princess, Jason of the Golden Fleece, shepherds and shepherdesses, and, of course, Bishop Blaise on horseback.

A eulogy was declaimed in praise of the bishop and the Yorkshire woollen industry and commerce – 'So let not Spain with us attempt to vie, Nor India's wealth pretend to soar so high' – sentiments repeated at intervals as this huge procession toured the main streets until 5 p.m.

ST LEGER STAKES

The oldest classic flat race for three-year-old thoroughbred colts and fillies was started on 24 September 1776 by Lt.-Col Anthony St Leger, and is run over a course of 1 mile, 6 furlongs and 132 yards (2,937m). It brought Doncaster to the fore, the grandstand having been designed by the now famous John Carr of York. Sir Tatton Sykes (1772-1863), the redoubtable 4th baronet of Sledmere, attended seventy-four St Legers. The event has been run every year except 1939, following the outbreak of the Second World War. Its heyday was in the 1920s, when the holiday week attracted 200,000 visitors.

Prior to railway travel, spectators, especially miners, had walked huge distances to Doncaster, even the eighteen miles from Sheffield, and walked back again the next day. Supporters were a very mixed company in the early days, with aristocrats, wealthy manufacturers, working men, thieves, animals on the loose and cattle being butchered in the streets.

ST MONDAY

Back in Tudor times Sheffield colliers had a 'sick day' for the town fair. In times much more recent, weekend drinking left many industrial workers feeling too tired to cope with that first shift afterwards. St Monday was a blessed bonus.

STOODLEY PIKE

Situated near the hamlet of Lumbutts, and on the Pennine Way, this Calder Valley landmark, built of local millstone grit, stands 120ft high, and 1,300ft above sea level. It began as a peace memorial, by public subscription, and as a tribute to the victorious Duke of Wellington, Napoleon having been was exiled to Elba in 1814. The original structure collapsed in a storm in 1854 and was rebuilt two years later at the end of the Crimean War.

STREET LIFE

The motor car has done much to erode the rich variety of street life. Up to the Second World War horse-drawn carts were commonplace. Enterprising householders gathered up manure to put on gardens, especially for rhubarb.

Vendors were legion. The milk man often called a twice a day, pouring pints, half-pints, even gills straight into kitchen jugs. During the late 1930s an Ackworth milkmaid carried two cans on a yoke. The Co-op cart, butcher, green-grocer, fish merchant came at least once a week. More casual were the pikelet woman, with her wicker basket; hot peas man; the ice-cream tricycle; and seasonally,

Stoodley Pike.

people like 'Watercress Wal' at Shipley. Spud Mick sold hot potatoes on Keighley's streets up to 1939.

Service providers included the coal merchant, chimney sweep, tinker and the occasional pedlar with his suitcase, and the knife and scissor man with his grinding wheel mounted on cart or tricycle. Eagerly awaited by youngsters were lamplighters, like Harold Ledger of Broadway (Pontefract) (who was also paid 'a tanner a tail' for rat catching).

Spasmodically there might turn up entertainers like the man with the dancing bear, or a monkey with an Italian owner; and up to the 1930s the tingalary or barrel organ activated by a handle.

Daring youngsters, usually boys, clung onto the back of carts, to be threatened if noticed with a cut from a horsewhip. Some begged pigs' bladders from a butcher to be blown up as footballs. Many lads enjoyed riding on bogeys – pram wheels fitted with a wooden plank or seat; or playing with water pistols or cap-firing revolvers, using dustbin lids as shields; or playing marbles in the gutter. On hot days road tar could be melted with a magnifying glass. Cold days brought out 'winter warmers' – big tins with holes pierced and filled with burning coke or coals, and fitted with a strong cord or strap so the warmer could be energetically whirled about. Snow and ice meant sliding, boys with studs on their boots creating sparks. Objects were placed on tramlines in Bradford to see the effect when squashed: bent pins held much promise. Piles of coats were improvised for goalposts, or a neighbour's dustbin borrowed for a wicket. Now and again they prospered – like Geoff Boycott, who played his first games in the alleys of Fitzwilliam before hitting 150 centuries for Yorkshire and England.

Girls liked ring games around a lamp post, or hop-scotch, pushing a doll's pram, or controlling a hoop with a stick. A skipping rope might go the width of the street. Some risque rhymes might be heard, but as a diversion there would be 'pitch, patch... pepper!' at which the rope would be turned very fast: this was known as pepping. 'All in – all out!' meant trying to enter or leave without fouling the rope.

There were plenty of small ball games, with various forms of rounders, like Pise Ball in Sheffield. There were all sorts of variations of hide and seek, relievo, kick the can – scatter – find. Big cans were threaded with cords to make stilts. There were high-jumping contests with stick or spar placed across two towers of housebricks, which were raised with each successful jump: never mind the scraped knees and painful falls. There was piggie-in-the-middle, and 'Statues' – identifying poses like 'You're a joiner/miner/ teacher/baker/thief!' There were occasions like Mummin' Neight in Keighley when children dressed up as film stars and did little acts to raise a few pence.

There was, of course, occasional mischief – knocking on doors or window tapping with a button on a thread. But children frequently were reprimanded by neighbours. This was an accepted part of communal discipline.

SUPERSTITIONS

There are so many. Old-time miners had a few: for some, washing the back too often was weakening.

There were ancient fears of a boggard, who could be a headless man, or a fearsome dog. Boggard Lane at Worrall near Oughtibridge is a reminder.

Avoid a peacock's tail feathers, with their circular markings: they betoken the evil eye!

TADCASTER STONE
Thievesdale Quarries was unfortunately named, for its Magnesian limestone was used to build such Christian centres as York Minster and Selby Abbey. Transportation problems were formidable. The stone had to be hauled by sled to Tadcaster, and then transferred to the Rivers Wharfe and Ouse: an epic job.

TANNER A WEEK MEDICAL INSURANCE
Especially in mining communities doctors were revered. In times of accidents they were called to the coal face. Soon after Dr Samuel Hodkinson came to Ryhill in 1919 he started a scheme of insurance for meeting medical bills. He was a popular if rather eccentric practitioner, pulling teeth, dispensing his own medicines, and running a dodgy car after some crises with a cycle and motorbike.

TEA AND T, VICAR?
A culinary delicacy after gelding was to fry lamb's testicles. Some farmers bit them off and spat them into the bowl.

TEMPLE MILL
Built between 1838-40, Temple Mill stands blackened and unloved in Marshall Street, Holbeck, Leeds. John Marshall, pioneer flax manufacturer, engaged Joseph Bonomi, specialist in Egyptian art and artefacts, as his designer. The columns and motifs

Temple Mill, Leeds.

Tenter post plaque.

Tenter post, Marsden.

were based on the Temple of Horus at Edfu, on the Nile. The chimney resembled Cleopatra's Needle. The mill was spacious and airy for its 1,000 workers, a grass roof helping to maintain equable temperatures below for flax spinning. At one time sheep grazed there – until one fell through!

TENTER

Daniel Defoe in his *Tour* (1724) commented that many Halifax dwellings were equipped with tenters. Washed and finished cloth was stretched to dry on tenter's wooden frames, or attached to sets of posts. Some remain yet on Warehouse Hill Road, Marsden, and the principle is recalled in names like Tenter Hill, Thurlstone and Tenter Meadow, Ecclesall. The expression 'on tenterhooks' derives from these times.

TODMORDEN TOWN HALL

Until local government changes in 1888, when the town was absorbed wholly into Yorkshire, the county boundary with Lancashire ran through it. This superb building was designed by John Gibson in 1870 in neo-classical style and funded by the mill-owning brothers Samuel, John and Joshua Fielden. The strikingly ornate pediment shows a classical frieze with, on the left, Lancashire cotton bales, and on the right sacks of Yorkshire wool and iron traders. On a central plinth sit two embracing women of the two counties.

TOFFEE KING

In 1891 John Mackintosh (1868-1920) experimented with a new confectionery recipe for his pastry shop. He wanted something between English (too hard) and American (too soft), and thoughtfully took down a pan given to himself and Violet as a wedding present to try out milkier flavours. The idea worked, they prospered and expanded, making Halifax into Toffee Town.

TOM PUDDINGS

Tom puddings were the creation of W.H. Bartholomew (1830-1919), chief engineer to the Aire and Calder Navigation Co. These square compartments (pans or puddings), each carrying around forty tons of coal, sailed in convoys or 'trains' from Knottingley to Goole. They were dubbed 'puddings' because on the canal they resembled a string of sausages – or Yorkshire puddings! By 1913 over a thousand were in service.

In the early decades they were driven by steam power, and later by diesel. Remarkably, the system begun in 1863 lasted until 1986; they were cheap and efficient, although there must have been a few scary moments as the tug men fortified themselves with

Pediment, Todmorden Town Hall.

A Tom Puddings 'Train' on the Aire and Calder Navigation. (Courtesy Yorkshire Waterways Museum)

beer for the thirty-mile journey. Generally, however, four men could control a train of up to thirty-eight puddings.

TOMBSTONE FEELERS

Both of the following men taught themselves to read, Braille fashion, by running childish fingers over tombstone letters. William Heaton, born in cottage next to Luddenden churchyard, worked as a handloom weaver, and later as a keeper of the People's Park, Halifax. He became a friend of Branwell Brontë and a poet of considerable merit.

Still more distinguished was Nicholas Saunderson (1682-1739), born at Thurlstone near Penistone, and blind from smallpox at the age of two. Yet he felt his way about Penistone churchyard, teaching himself letters, names and words. Despite all his handicaps, he attended the local grammar school, proceeding to Cambridge, first as student, then in 1707 as teacher, dealing with Newton's Optics. Later he became Lucasian Professor of Mathematics, a post once held by Newton himself.

TONIC-SOL-FA

This system of sight singing, substituting syllables for notes (do, reh, me, fah, so) was adapted from work by Sarah Ann Glover of Norwich, and popularised in the 1860s by the Revd John Curwen (1816-80) of Heckmondwike. It was well received by conductors of West Yorkshire choirs.

T'OWD TRUMPET

This was the affectionate nickname given to the Revd Henry Venn (1725-1797), charismatic vicar of St Peter's, Huddersfield from 1759 to 1771, and a founder of the Clapham Sect, an influential evangelical group in the Church of England. His example became known to reformers like Wilberforce and Lord Shaftesbury. His shrewd anecdotes drew the crowds, classes for converts were well subscribed, disruptive elements were overcome and he achieved a great change in the moral climate. He stopped Sunday trading and Sunday animal slaughter. His supporters, 'Venn people', enforced the Sabbath peace.

At the funeral of William Grimshaw at St Mary's, Luddenden, in 1763, he preached the sermon. Before leaving the parish he handed his successor two lists – the poor and the very poor. In quieter Huntingdonshire he partially recovered from consumption.

TURNPIKES AND TOLLS

From the latter part of the seventeenth century, with the increase of wheeled traffic, turnpike trusts levied tolls in order to maintain a defined length of road. The first West Yorkshire turnpike, from Halifax to Rochdale, was completed in 1735. Leeds to Otley followed in 1755; and Sheffield to Leeds three years later, passing through Barnsley and Wakefield.

The toll house, where the collector lived, was placed at road junctions, or jutted into the roadway. Strategically placed windows gave vantage points to check arriving traffic. Local carts and funeral hearses were generally exempt of tolls. Among toll houses remaining are the octagonal three-storeyed Barber Fields Cupola house at Ringinglow, Sheffield; the Scarcroft toll house (Leeds) at the end of Thorner Lane; and Bar House between Otley and Bramhope.

Inevitably there was much opposition to these new barriers to free trade, and many stratagems to avoid payment, like an organised rush of several to get through at once. In June 1753 there were violent protests to the turnpike at Harewood Bridge. Forewarned, Lord Lascelles had 300 tenants ready to repel the rioters. Thirty prisoners were taken and ten jailed.

A week later a carter refusing to pay the toll at the Beeston turnpike was arrested by soldiers. He was rescued from jail by a determined mob, which tore up paving stones to break into the Old King's Arms, Briggate, Leeds. The Riot Act was read and soldiers brought in. Eight rioters were killed and forty were wounded.

TURPIN LEGEND

Dick Turpin has been romanticised as a handsome rogue and a daring highwayman. More active in the East Riding, he was captured at the Green Dragon, Welton and hanged on the Knavesmire, York – where he threw himself off the scaffold on 7 April 1739.

Above: Stone from Nicholas Saunderson's birthplace - ('Here was born…'). The tablet is built into a wall at the junction of Manchester Road and Towngate, Thurlstone.

Right: Saunderson Memorial, St John's Gardens, Penistone Churchyard. Created by Sarah Jones-Morris and children of Spring Vale Primary School.

One local legend is worth repeating. When he was staying at an inn at Cantley (Doncaster) in 1738 the landlord informed the authorities. Turpin went back and cut his tongue out – hence 'Warning Tongue Lane'.

UMBRELLA MAN

After setting up a wire-drawing business at Stocksbridge, Samuel Fox (1815-87) began experimenting with string steel. In this part of the Peak District, where rain clouds regularly gather, he turned his attention to creating a steel-ribbed umbrella (1852), the prototype of the Paragon frame which was successful for many decades. He also adapted light steel frames for crinoline dresses.

UNION SECESSIONISTS

Rugby League began with the secession of twelve clubs from the Yorkshire Rugby Union over the question of compensation for loss of wages incurred by working-class players. The Union remained uncompromising on amateur status for all of its clubs. At a meeting held at the George Hotel, Huddersfield on 29 August 1895, twenty-one northern clubs (twelve Yorkshire, nine Lancashire) voted twenty to one to secede from the Rugby Football Union to set up a Northern Rugby Football Union, which became Rugby Football League in 1922. Accordingly, players became full or part-time professionals. The hotel has an excellent exhibition of League memorabilia.

A former Rugby professional, David Storey, born in Wakefield, wrote his first novel, *This Sporting Life* (1960), about a young aggressive player, Frank Machin, whose romantic life was less successful. It is a reminder that even successful sportsmen are vulnerable to time and injury – and fame, which may be hard to handle off the field.

UNSENTIMENTAL JOURNEY

Herbert Scarborough was a sensitive Queensbury lad whose train journey to Keighley Grammar School was often accompanied by assorted industrial females, clad in paint-daubed dungarees, who smoked, swore, shouted, sang and teased, terrifying him, as he recorded in his diary. A particular horror was a long tunnel in whose dark recesses he was wont to be lifted onto their knees, suffering their cigarette smoke and intrusive embraces.

One Bradford mills' ritual, known as 'sunning', encouraged rumbustious female operatives to seize a new lad and 'sun' him by pulling his trousers down.

UPWARDS REVERSE

At South Elmshall in the early twentieth century a milkman called Barlow in a Model T van couldn't climb Elmsall Hill in forward gear – so he reversed up.

URINE

For centuries, urine – or lant, as it was called in the trade – was a vital ingredient in removing grease during the scouring of wool. Loom workers were invited to pee into a bucket that did regular rounds in the mills. Animal urine was sprinkled on the cloth, which was then trampled (or 'walked') bare-footed, scoured and hung up to dry. Later this natural cleansing agent was replaced by distilled ammonia.

'Stale urine is so called because, in the process of manufacture, cloth is weeted with that liquid when sent to the mill, the object being to bring out the grease. Weeting is also called lecking. I have been told of persons using this substance instead of soap, even for washing themselves'. (Alfred Easther: *Glossary of Almondbury and Huddersfield*, 1883.)

Some enthusiasts believed that urine was good for skin, wrinkles, chapped hands and reducing warts.

It occasionally had a social function – to be emptied by the doors of blackguards and illicit lovers.

VACCINATION OPPOSED

The Keighley Board of Guardians opposed the vaccination of children, regarding recent Acts of Parliament as tyrannical. Support, always ready, grew further. On 10 August 1876 John Jeffrey was arrested, and his colleagues the following day. They were imprisoned in the Devonshire Hotel. When a mob fought their way in, officers transferred the prisoners to a horse-bus. The crowd took it over. Incarcerated in York Castle, the Guardians were seen as martyrs, and on the 8 September they were freed. While this particular case eventually petered out, public doubts about the efficacy and wisdom of vaccination continued for many years, both in Keighley and nationwide – despite continuing deaths from smallpox.

VANDALISM

During Henry VIII's suppression of the monasteries, in 1537, the choir stalls in Roche Abbey were smashed to kindle fires to melt lead taken from the roof.

VEHICLES

Excessive speed: 'It was stated in evidence yesterday that the engine of one car was running at the rate of 12 miles an hour, a pace certainly too great to be tolerated in the town.' (*Bradford Daily Telegraph*, 28 August 1884.)

VERMUYDEN

In 1626, Cornelius Vermuyden (1590-1677), a Dutch engineer who had already reclaimed land in the Thames area, was invited by King Charles I (as lord of four local manors) to drain flood-prone Hatfield Chase. The southern branch of the River Don was closed, and its waters diverted to the northern arm, the new 'Dutch River'

Clifford's Tower, and the entrance to York Castle.

opening directly into the Ouse at Goole, and so on to the Humber. But different areas, like Sykehouse and Fishlake, suffered from flooding. There were protests also at the loss of the southerly Don: for some farmers it had been beneficial. Riots broke out, with the destruction of embankments. Some Dutch workmen were drowned in their dykes by local foresters. When the Civil War broke out in 1642 the Dutch naturally supported the king, and local men the Roundheads.

VERSATILITY

In later Victorian times one-armed Bill Saunderson, postman of Stainton, rang the church bells by using his remaining arm and looping a rope around each foot. And 'Woody Leg', a Keighley hot-pea vendor, reputedly stirred his peas with his wooden leg.

VICE

In the mid-1840s the new incumbent at St James church, off Kirkgate, Leeds, the Revd J. Slatter, wrote: 'I had given me by the police a list of the brothels in my district, and I was horrified to find that, in a circle of a hundred yards, of which my room was the centre, there were no less than thirteen of such dens'.

VIRGIN VIADUCT

Under the auspices of the York and North Midland Railway this attractive eleven-arched structure over the River Wharfe at Tadcaster was built in 1849 by the Railway King, George Hudson. But when his fortunes waned, the proposed Leeds to York line was not built. The viaduct remained unconnected until 1882; after this it was utilised, until 1955, to carry a siding to a mill on the east side of the river.

VISITORS

In 1693 Celia Fiennes, intrepid horsewoman, riding side-saddle, reported of the Castleford area: 'The greatest danger to travellers is from Coale Pits close to the Highway'. She had a happier view of Leeds streets, with fine stone buildings, but regretted missing the market-day treat – meat or cheese which came free when ale was ordered.

John Wesley described Barnsley as 'a place famous for all manner of wickedness'. More happily of Bradford: 'None behaved indecently but the curate of the parish'. And of Huddersfield: 'A wilder people I never saw in England, the men, women and children filled the street as we rode along and appeared just ready to devour us. They were, however, tolerably quiet while I preached, only a few pieces of dirt were thrown'. (Journal, June 1757.)

Contrast Friedrich Engels *re* Huddersfield's buildings: 'the handsomest by far of all the factory towns in Yorkshire… by reason of its charming situation and modern architecture'.

Defoe noted that Doncaster was a great manufacturing town, 'principally for knitting'. He paid tribute to the assiduity of countryside workers near Halifax – 'women and children always busy carding, spinning, etc. so that no hands being unemployed, all can gain their bread, even from the youngest to the ancient; scarce anything above four years old but its hands were sufficient for its own support.' Barnsley, he noted, was grimy and smokey, 'as if they were all smiths that lived in it'. Reputedly Defoe wrote part of *Robinson Crusoe* while staying at the Rose and Crown Inn, Halifax, 1719. Sheffield's houses were 'dark and black, occasioned by the continued smoke of the forges, which are always at work' (1720).

Virgin Viaduct, Tadcaster.

A century on William Cobbett agreed: 'Nothing can be conceived more grand or more terrible than the yellow waves of fire that instantly issue from the tops of the furnaces.' (Sheffield.)

VOLUNTEER BUSES

In October 1940, during the Blitz, London transport appealed for help. Halifax was the first to respond by sending two Park Royal Regent buses. Soon afterwards Leeds City Transport sent south a fleet of twelve AEC Regents. Nearly five years later representative vehicles took a proud part in the victory procession.

WAINHOUSE TOWER

It has been dubbed 'Tower of Spite,' and 'Rich Man's Folly'. Standing loftily on a rural island at Wakefield Gate, Halifax, it was the creation, in 1871, of John Edward Wainhouse; he meant it to serve his dyeworks on Washer Lane, though there are doubts whether the smoke would have escaped. A curious quarrel had been waged with a neighbour, Sir Henry Edwards, each building a higher fence against the other. Did Wainhouse build the tower to spy on him? The observation platform on top lends credence to this possibility.

There was trouble at the tower's planning stage. After a dispute between Isaac Booth, the original designer, and Wainhouse, Richard Dugdale took over. Stone-built, octagonal and crowned with ornate balconies, the tower stands 254ft tall. There are 403 steps in the spiral staircase. The building is occasionally opened to the public.

WALTON CALVES

Here was a dismissive name for a past generation of Walton men (near Wetherby) who failed to arrest the notorious highwaymen, Swift Nick Nevison. Theoretically this looked an easy task, as he was asleep by a well. However, Nick's quick wits saved him, for when he seized a stick and pointed it at them, they let him escape.

CHARLES WATERTON (1782-1865)

Eccentric extraordinaire, intrepid traveller, pioneer naturalist... so many tales are told of this gifted but peculiar individual. As a schoolboy at Stonyhurst he became official rat-catcher. His scientific writings, especially on South America, were of interest to Darwin. He rode on an alligator's back and bound a poisonous snake's jaw with his braces in order to take a toxic sample.

Back home at Walton Hall, Wakefield, he established (in all probability) the first nature reserve in the world in 1820. He invented the bird nesting-box. A practical joker, he joined together spare parts of animals to make grotesques. Himself a Roman Catholic, Waterton made some of his fanciful creations to look like VIP Protestants: a monkey with horns and donkey's ears resembled Martin Luther. In 1817 he placed a glove on the lightning conductor on St Peter's, Rome; Pope Pius VII persuaded him to remove it.

Wainhouse Tower, Halifax.

Charles Waterton.

He sometimes bounded on all fours, barking to greet visitors. He once dissected a gorilla after dinner. A penitent in later years, especially after his young wife Anne died in childbirth, he retired at eight o'clock, sleeping on the floor and rising for prayers at midnight.

He wore loose-fitting clothes, and slit vents in his hats. Frugal in general, he nevertheless kept a fire going in all seasons, often lighting one outside.

Waterton believed in letting his own blood, or 'tapping the claret'. Agile in old age, he was still climbing trees at eighty.

WAY OF THE WORLD

Like so many Yorkshire writers, William Congreve (1670-1729) soon deserted his native village – in his case, Bardsey, where he was christened on 10 February 1670. To seek one's fortune elsewhere is but the way of the world – the title of one of his famous plays. His father was an army officer, so they had to move as ordered. Even though he never returned to his birthplace, so many of Congreve's famous lines resonate: 'Courtship to marriage, as a very witty prologue to a very dull play'; 'the good received, the giver is forgot.'

WEDDINGS

In many places (eg Stainton and Wilsden) the church gates were tied until local children received acceptable coins from the newly-wed groom. Occasional conflicts arose. On 24 November 1617 at Cawthorne, some boys, dissatisfied with an offer, kept the unhappy couple locked in, resulting in a Consistory Court action, York – the outcome of which is unrecorded.

Wedding races from the church to pub, or the bride's home, were commonplace. At Yeadon unwed men raced to the Robin Hood Inn, the first arrival receiving a full tankard, adorned with ribbon. Another popular custom was for the winner to retrieve the bride's garter, specially embroidered. Coy brides might offer a ribbon instead. Some couples left on one horse, scattering coins for the youngsters.

Not all artefacts have been auspicious. In St Mary's church, Spotborough, are sixteenth century pew ends representing before and after marriage. 'Before' shows two heads facing; 'after' has them looking in opposite directions. Congreve would have understood!

WELCOMING A NEWBORN

Typical ceremonial gifts for a newborn child were an egg (hopefully conferring fertility); salt (health); bread (basic necessity); and a silver coin (wishing wealth or luck). In the Calder valley in hard times a more immediate neighbourly response might be to bring in a small helping of gruel.

WENTWORTH FOLLIES

The east façade (606ft) of Wentworth House makes it the longest country house in Europe. The estate was once the stately home of the Marquis of Rockingham and the Earls Fitzwilliam: Thomas Wentworth, Earl of Strafford, adviser to King Charles I, was executed in 1641; Charles, 2nd Marquis of Rockingham, was twice Whig Prime minister (1765-6 and 1782).

Among the estate's interesting follies are:

The Hoober Stand, a hill-top pyramid, 100ft high, in honour of George II and commemorating the Jacobite defeat of 1746.

Slightly higher and designed by John Carr in 1778, Keppel's Column was built to mark the acquittal of Admiral Keppel, friend of the 2nd Marquis, court marshalled for failing to arrest French warships at Ushant.

The Needle's Eye, built about 1740, is associated with a legend of the 2nd Marquis wagering he could drive a horse and carriage 'through the eye of a needle' (i.e. the archway of this 48ft high stone pyramid).

Needle's Eye, Wentworth.

WHAT A WAY TO GO!

John Mitchell, first owner, fond of a drink and dare, jumped with improvised wings off an escarpment behind Scout Hall, near Halifax (c. 1680). The wings failed and he was killed.

In 1771 some members of the notorious Cragg Vale coiners were present in a Heptonstall pub when a local labourer, Abraham Ingham, boasted of what he knew of the murder of Dighton, the late Excise Man. They tipped him upside down and thrust his head into the bar-room fire, clapped red-hot tongs around his neck and tipped burning coals down his trousers.

A puzzling epitaph in All Saints churchyard, Darfield, Barnsley reads: 'The mortal remains of Robert Millthorp who died September 13th 1826 aged 19. He lost his life by inadvertently throwing this stone upon himself whilst in the service of James Raymond of Ardsley, who erected it in his memory.'

In November 1853 Martha Weldon, house servant of Whiston, Rotherham, and bridesmaid at a friend's wedding, danced far into the night. The next day she fell dead from her chair. A coroner's jury found that she died from apoplexy due to excessive dancing. (*Leeds Mercury*, 18 November 1853.)

On 13 October 1905 Sir Henry Irving, playing *Becket* (by Tennyson), was taken ill in the Theatre Royal, Bradford after uttering the line 'Into thy hands, O Lord'. He died that night in the Midland Hotel with his manager, Bram Stoker (of *Dracula* fame), by his bedside.

The body of 40-stone Robert Cutforthay had to be lowered into his coffin by block and tackle. A memorial tablet, 1905, is located in the north aisle of All Saints church, Rotherham.

Twenty-one year old Lily Cove died when her parachute failed to open at a gala at Haworth on 11 June 1906.

WHIT WALKS, PARADES AND PROCESSIONS

Charlotte Brontë wrote about them in her novel, *Shirley* (1849). Whitsuntide has traditionally brought Whit Walks in West Yorkshire. Led by a band and banner bearers, church and chapel members proceeded through the streets, boys in best suits, girls dressed in white. They may stop at intervals to sing hymns, lead on to the market place, or return to their place of worship for a service. In the afternoon there are sports and a tea. Their heyday was in Victorian times, but they are still popular.

Whit Monday Sings in Sheffield's Firth Park attracted thousands up to 1939. At other times hundreds of people have attended Friendly Society processions, Sunday schools, summer galas, children's treats, miners' rallies and demonstrations, Jubilee processions (1887 and 1897) and coronation celebrations. When Earl Fitzwilliam laid the foundation stone of Huddersfield Railway Station in 1846 there were processions and a public holiday.

Prior to the National Health Service, many local events (parades, floats, competitions) were held to raise funds for hospitals. Ecclesfield, for instance, used to favour fancy-dress parades, especially animals and swans.

WILL OF WILLIAM ROKEBY

Rokeby was rector of St Oswald's, Sandal Parva (now Kirk Sandall) from 1487 to 1502 and later vicar of St John the Baptist church, Halifax; and eventually (1511) Archbishop of Dublin. He officiated at the baptism of Mary Tudor in 1516. He died in 1521. Under the provisions of his will, his bowels were to be buried in Dublin, his heart in Halifax and his body in Sandal Parva. A chapel was to be built over each. At St John's the chapel is on the north side. At St Oswald's it is in the north-east corner with a monument to Rokeby.

WITCHES

One source of anti-witch sentiment was the Biblical injunction, 'Thou shalt not suffer a witch to live' (Exodus xxii, v.18) During the thirteenth century Archbishops of York ordered all church fonts to be covered and locked in order to stop people stealing Holy Water to counteract witches' spells. An Act of 1543 made witchcraft a felony, and persecution was encouraged by King James I.

Mary Pannell, a maid at Ledston Hall, offered a lotion for her mistress to rub the chest of her young son; the boy drank it and died. Mary, accused of witchcraft, was tried at York, and burnt at Castleford in 1603.

Mary Sykes, the Witch of Bolling, was acquitted at an assize trial in 1650; she had been accused of bewitching horses, and having tell-tale lumps on her bottom and left side.

Catherine Earle of Rothwell was brought before a court at York Castle in 1655 on charges of having put spells on a man called Frank, killing him; and causing a former employer – and lover – Henry Hatfield to waste away for many months. Mrs Hatfield helped to promote the charge, impressed, no doubt, by the likelihood that her husband

A witch feeding her familiars (old print).

had fathered Mrs Earle's daughter, Anne. Despite an allegation of having 'the likeness of a pap' on her body, Catherine Earle was acquitted.

There were instances of witches in gainful employment. At Esholt in the seventeenth century the Lingbob witch, Hannah Gordon, became rich, with rumoured wealth of £1,000.

Often harmless old women – such as Martha Watts of eighteenth-century Barnsley, the subject of gossip and innuendo – were scapegoats for any local misfortune, such as illnesses or poor crops. Still, Martha lived into her nineties.

There may be justice in the claim that witches made women beauty-conscious, via preparations of natural materials (leaves, strawberries, dandelion juice, onions, walnut oil, honey of roses etc). A white witch might be sought for a herbal remedy, a love potion or fortune-telling. John Steward was found guilty at Leeds Assizes in 1719 of selling love potions to young women, but strong public opinion helped to free him.

Certain fortune tellers gained a considerable reputation – and pocket money. At Wibsey Jenny Milner attracted clients of a wide social range, outlining their destiny through tea leaves and coffee grains.

Mountain ash or rowan tree branches were supposed to keep evil spirits away. Some folk pinned cuttings on their clothes before going out. Other deterrents included a silver thimble buried inside a building, and stones with holes in them to hang over doorways and barns.

WOMEN'S OPPORTUNITIES IN BRADFORD

The suffragette movement was represented in West Yorkshire, not least in Bradford. Lilian Armitage, Secretary of the Bradford Women's Social and Political Union, joined with the Pankhursts to lead a march on Parliament in February 1907, obstructing the police in order to gain publicity for the cause. She spent fourteen days in Holloway prison, not in vain, for the vote was extended in 1918 to women of thirty years of age, provided they were householders or married to householders. In the same year Mrs Annie Arnold became the first woman to be elected to Bradford City Council. Two years later Kathleen Chambers was elected, becoming the first woman alderman in 1924.

WOOLLEN SHROUDS

To revive a struggling woollen industry, the Burial in Wool Act (1667) required that the dead, except plague victims, should be buried in English woollen shrouds. According to Methley church records, 'John Townend was buried 30 of March 1667, this was the first that was buried in woolan'.

But at Harthill, 'Received April 7th 1789 of ye undertaker, at ye Funeral of ye Duke of Leeds, a moiety of penalty for burying in linnen of £2 10s 0d.'

Thomas, 4th Duke of Leeds died at Kiveton Hall, and was buried in the family vault in Harthill church.

Coffins were once optional. At Bramham church shortly after the 1667 Act the burial fee was two shillings with a coffin, or eighteen pence without. As elsewhere a parish coffin was available for the poor – to be returned to the church after conveying the deceased to the graveside.

WORKHOUSE WOES

In the notorious case of the Huddersfield scandal of 1848 a report showed that typhus was rife; that inmates shared beds with the dead and dying; and that beds were lice-ridden, with linen unchanged for nine weeks.

After the 1834 Poor Law Amendment Act there were many deliberate privations. At Otley the elderly were required to sit on backless benches to emphasise their 'less eligibility'.

Like many prisons, Keighley Workhouse had cells fitted with crank mills, some 8,800 turns being needed to grind four bushels of corn.

WORLD'S SMALLEST MAN?

This was surely Edwin Calvert, buried in the south-east corner of Christ church, Skipton. Under 36in tall and weighing only twenty-three and a half pounds, he was known, with wry humour, as 'Commander-in-Chief'. Edwin liked to spend time in his cousin John's shoemaker's shop in the High Street. He was only seventeen when he died on 7 August 1859.

YEADON HAIL

During a freak storm at Yeadon on 2 July 1968 roads were blocked by several feet of hailstones.

YORKSHIRE PENNY BANK

The inspiration started with a sermon by the Revd Charles Kingsley in Whitehall Chapel on 12 March 1856 on the profligacy of London unfortunates. In the congregation was Edward Akroyd, a Halifax mill owner who determined to encourage thrift in his workers. The idea of regularly investing a copper or two started almost immediately in East Parade, Leeds, soon becoming the West Riding Penny

Brontë Museum sign, Haworth.

Savings Bank – and from 1860 the Yorkshire Penny Bank. Facilities were provided in mechanics institutes (Castleford 1860), in pubs and church halls, and, from 1874, in schools. Cheque books were issued to small tradesmen from 1872. When Akroyd gave up the presidency in 1878 there were over 100,000 members.

As a change from 'guesting' in other premises, the Yorkshire Penny Bank at Haworth in May 1895 offered its top floor to accommodate the first Brontë Museum. Nowadays the building is occupied by the Tourist Information Centre. Such were the beginnings of the Yorkshire Bank.

YORKSHIRE PUD HERESY

Unity amongst Yorkshire folk is generally expected, especially against off-comed-uns (outsiders), but differences of opinion have been expressed on this most indispensable icon of identity. We all know – don't we? – that Yorkshire Pudding is central to a hefty dinner with beef, potatoes, piles of vegetables and lashings of gravy. Yet within these Broad Acres, and especially in the south around Sheffield and Doncaster, there have been – are – desperate folk using the Pud as a dessert, with butter, sugar, treacle, raspberry vinegar and other such sweet, unsavoury rammel!

YOUNGEST TEACHER?

At St Peter's Catholic School, Doncaster in 1897, an inspector found a seven-year-old girl in sole charge of thirty-five babies in the gallery, trying to teach them arithmetic.

ZEALOUS PEDANT

Son of a Leeds cloth merchant, antiquarian Ralph Thoresby (1658-1725) kept a diary from 1677, describing buildings, earthworks, sermons, epitaphs, coins, eggs, plants, bones, rare Bibles, family trees and much else. He was constantly adding artefacts to the museum inherited from his father. He had an eye for oddities, like the Dorset man apparently eating hot brimstone, wax and lead. In 1697 he was elected Fellow of the Royal Society for his studies of Roman remains, and was Leeds' first historian, publishing in 1715 a *Ducatus Leodiensis*.

Yet he recognised daily stresses and strains, as these extracts show:

> 'We found the way very deep, and in some places dangerous for a coach that we walked on foot.' (*Journey to York*, 1708.)
> 'Read and wrote all day, save usual attendance at church. Evening had company of brother Thoresby's children to close up the year; was disturbed with foolish or rather sinful mummers, and was perhaps too zealous to repress them. Lord pity and pardon.' (Diary of Ralph Thoresby FRS, 31 December 1713.)

The museum did not long survive his death. To perpetuate his memory the Thoresby Society was established in 1889

ZEPPELIN RAID

The raid of 25 September 1916 by German Naval Zeppelin L22 shocked Sheffield and the nation. Thirty-six incendiary and high explosive bombs were dropped between Burngreave and Darnal, killing twenty-eight people, and injuring nineteen. Anti-aircraft defenders were said to have been at a ball at the Grand Hotel. Extra searchlights were brought in, but street lamps, blacked out halfway down, went out only during buzzer alerts, and shops shut at 8.00 instead of 11.00 p.m.

By the Second World War, despite the blackout of street and house lighting enforced by air-raid wardens, the Luftwaffe could hardly mistake the massive industrial infrastructure, steelworks, forges, furnaces and railways below. The Blitz on the city, especially of December 1940, remains an awesome memory for the oldest generation.

One that didn't get away: the wreckage of a zeppelin brought down in Essex (*Illustrated London News*).

Bibliography

M. Campbell, *Curious Tales of Old West Yorkshire* (Sigma Press, 1999)

R. and M. Freethy, *Discovering Inland Yorkshire* (J. Donald, 1992)

M. Hartley & J. Ingilby, *Yorkshire Portraits* (JM. Dent & Sons Ltd., 1961)

M. Hartley & J. Ingilby, *Life and Tradition in West Yorkshire* (Smith Settle, 1990)

*The Hidden Places of Yorkshire – South East and West (*M and M Publishing, 1990)

N.A. Ibbotson, *Exploring West Yorkshire's History* (Breedon Books, 2008)

A. Kellett, *Know Your Yorkshire* (Dalesman 1980)

A. Kellett, *The Yorkshire Dictionary of Dialect, Tradition and Folklore* (Smith Settle, 1994)

W. R. Mitchell, *Yorkshire Mill Town Traditions* (Dalesman, 1978)

N. Rhea, *Yorkshire Days* (Hutton Press, 1995)

H.J. Scott, *Yorkshire Heritage* (Robert Hale, 1970)

I. Shannon, *Infamous Yorkshire Women* (Sutton Publishing, 2007)

Duncan & Trevor Smith, *South and West Yorkshire Curiosities* (Dovecote Press, 1992)

Julia Smith, *Fairs, Feasts and Frolics* (Smith Settle, 1989)

Ivor Smullen, *Yorkshire Pie* (Fort Publishing, 2001)

South and West Yorkshire Federation of Women's Institutes, *South and West Yorkshire Village Book* (Countryside Books, 1991)

South Yorkshire County Council, *Discovering South Yorkshire* (Shire Publications, Ltd., 1975)

John Spencer, *Towns and villages of Britain – West Yorkshire* (Sigma Press, 2000)

P. Thomas, *Yorkshire's Historic Pubs* (Sutton Publishing Ltd., 2005)

R. Woodhouse, *Curiosities of West Yorkshire* (Sutton, 2007)

Other titles published by The History Press

West Yorkshire Folk Tales
JOHN BILLINGSLEY

Whether hailing from the open Pennine hills or the close-knit neighbourhoods of the industrial towns, the people of West Yorkshire have always been fond of a good story. Within these pages are tales of tragic love affairs, thwarted villainy, witches, fairies, hidden treasure and much more. The intriguing stories, brought to life with beautiful line-drawings by a local artist, will be enjoyed by readers time and again.

978 0 7524 5292 0

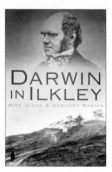

Olde Yorkshire Punishments
HOWARD PEACH

This fascinating volume explores the darkest aspects of crime and punishment in Yorkshire over the centuries - a history by turns gruesome, intriguing and strange. From the stocks, joug and branding iron to the prison cell, galley - and noose - every punishment that could befall the criminals of Yorkshire is included in this volume. With sections on Church scandals, why bull baiting was a legal requierment and the use of the Sharp Maiden - the guillotine - it will delight anyone with an interest in Yorkshire's penal history.

978 0 7524 4661 5

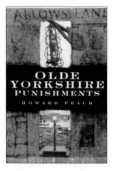

Darwin in Ilkley
MIKE DIXON & GREGORY RADICK

When *On the Origin of Species* was published on 24 November 1859, its author, Charles Darwi was near the end of a nine-week stay in Ilkley. He had come for the 'water cure' - a regime of cold baths and wet sheets - and for relaxation. But he used his time in Ilkley to shore up support, through extensive correspondence, for the extraordinary theory that the *Origin* would put before the world: evolution by natural selection. Mike Dixon and Gregory Radick bring to life Victorian Ilkley and the dramas of body and mind that marked Darwin's visit.

978 0 7524 5283 8

Mrs Hibbert's Pick Me Up and Other Recipies from a Yorkshire Dale
JOANNA MOODY

Joanna Dawson, a dairy farmer, local historian and Methodist preacher, combined her religious faith with a delight in the local traditions of agriculture and domestic affairs in the Yorkshire Dales. Hers is a fragrant scene from the farmhouse kitchens of long ago, when large teas and suppers were the reward for a hard-working rural life. The book is also richly illustrated with pen and ink drawings and photographs taken in the Dales a century ago.

978 0 7524 5728 4

Visit our website and discover thousands of other History Press books.
www.thehistorypress.co.uk

The History Press